AF333483

IMPORTANT BILLING AND CREDIT REQUIREMENTS

All producers of OLYMPUS ON MY MIND *must* give credit to the Authors of the Work in all programs distributed in connection with performances of the Work, and in all instances in which the title of the Work appears for the purposes of advertising, publicizing or otherwise exploiting a production thereof; including, without limitation to, programs, souvenir books and playbills. The names of the Authors *must* also appear on a separate line in which no other matter appears, immediately following the title of the Work, and *must* be in size of type not less than 50% of the size of type used for the title of the Work. Billing *must* be substantially as follows:

(Name of Producer)
presents

"OLYMPUS ON MY MIND"

Book and Lyrics by   Music by
BARRY HARMAN   **GRANT STURIALE**

Original production
Directed by
BARRY HARMAN

Originally presented by
Harve Brosten and Mainstage Productions, Ltd.

PROGRAM NOTES:

All programs for OLYMPUS ON MY MIND, and all posters, *must* list the following:

(NAME OF PRODUCER OR
PRODUCING ORGANIZATION)

in association with

"MURRAY THE FURRIER"

present

OLYMPUS ON MY MIND

In addition, all programs *must* carry the following bio:

"MURRAY THE FURRIER" (*Co-Producer*) is Murray Sands in real life. Though this is his first venture as a theatrical producer, his face is familiar to local TV audiences for his late night appearances on the famous "Murray the Furrier" commercials. Murray has been dealing in used furs at his store on Avenue J in Brooklyn for over 40 years. He met his lovely new wife Delores on a recent trip to Lake Tahoe, where she was appearing in a local niterie. Murray has three lovely grandchildren—Adam, Allison and Joshua—of whom he is extremely proud. He also has a daughter, Joanne, to whom he no longer speaks.

Lastly, all programs *must* contain a full-page ad, with the following:

DELORES—BREAK A LEG!

Congratulations on our 3 Month Anniversary

Love, "Murray the Furrier"

"Don't Dream About A Fur, Wear One of Mine"

At Avenue J in Brooklyn for over 40 years

NOTE TO PRODUCERS

Many audience members familiar with mythology may wonder why, if the play is set in Ancient Greece, the gods JUPITER and MERCURY are referred to by their Roman names.

For that reason, the following program note should also be included in all programs for the play:

> The legend of Amphitryon, which chronicles the birth of Hercules, has been used as source material by dramatists down through the ages. Playwright Jean Giradoux reckoned his version of the story was the 38th to have been written.
>
> The musical play you will see tonight is suggested by a version written by German Romantic playwright Heinrich Von Kleist in 1807. Kleist's play was modeled after a play by Moliere, which was in turn adapted from a number of other plays, including one by Plautus.
>
> In all cases, the dramatists referred to the two Greek gods in the story (Zeus and Hermes) by their more familiar Roman names (Jupiter and Mercury). The authors of *Olympus On My Mind* have chosen to follow in that tradition.

Finally, the role of AMPHITRYON, although played by the same actor who plays JUPITER, should be listed in programs as being played by a fictitious actor (the original production used the name "George Spelvin").

LAMB'S THEATRE

HARVE BROSTEN
and
MAINSTAGE PRODUCTIONS, LTD.

in association with
"MURRAY THE FURRIER"

present

OLYMPUS ON MY MIND
A New Musical

Suggested by "Amphitryon" by Heinrich Von Kleist

Book and Lyrics by   *Music by*
BARRY HARMAN   **GRANT STURIALE**

Starring

MARTIN VIDNOVIC

PEGGY HEWETT   **ELIZABETH AUSTIN**   **JASON GRAAE**   **EMILY ZACHARIAS**

and **LEWIS J. STADLEN**

KEITH BENNETT   **PETER KAPETAN**   **DANNY WEATHERS**

Set Design by   *Costume Design by*   *Lighting Design by*
CHRISTOPHER STAPLETON   **STEVEN JONES**   **FABIAN YEAGER**

Press Representative   *General Management*
HENRY LUHRMAN ASSOCIATES   **HORNER/STUART ENTERPRISES**

Production Consultant   *Assistant Director*   *Production Stage Manager*
JAY S. BULMASH   **EDWARD MARSHALL**   **JOSEPH A. ONORATO**

Choreography
PAMELA SOUSA

Directed by
BARRY HARMAN

The Lamb's Theatre is operated by the Lamb's Theatre Company Ltd.,
Carolyn Rossi Copeland, Executive Director

CAST
(in order of appearance)

The Chorus
   Tom .... PETER KAPETAN
   Dick .... DANNY WEATHERS
   Horace .... KEITH BENNETT
   Delores .... ELIZABETH AUSTIN
Jupiter (aka Jove, Zeus)* .... MARTIN VIDNOVIC
Mercury* .... JASON GRAAE
Charis .... PEGGY HEWETT
Alcmene .... EMILY ZACHARIAS
Sosia .... LEWIS J. STADLEN
Amphitryon .... GEORGE SPELVIN

Standby for Jupiter/Amphitryon—Mark Zimmerman
UNDERSTUDIES
Understudies never substitute for listed players unless a specific announcement
for the appearance is made at the time of the performance.

For Mercury and Sosia—Paul Kassel; Alcmene, Charis and Delores—Nancy Johnston; Tom
Dick, Horace and Swing—Bruce Moore.

The play is set in the ancient Greek city of Thebes, during the course of a 41-hour day.

* The legend of Amphitryon, which chronicles the birth of Hercules, has been used as source
material by dramatists down through the ages. Playwright Jean Giradoux reckoned his version of the story was the 38th to have been written.

The musical play you will see tonight is suggested by a version written by German Romantic
playwright Heinrich von Kleist in 1807. Kleist's play was modeled after a play by Molière,
which was in turn adapted from a number of other plays, including one by Plautus.

In all cases, the dramatists referred to the two Greek gods in the story (Zeus and Hermes)
by their more familiar, Roman names (Jupiter and Mercury). The authors of *Olympus on
My Mind* have chosen to follow in that tradition.

MUSICAL NUMBERS
ACT I

"Welcome to Greece" .... CHORUS
"Heaven on Earth" .... JUPITER, ALCMENE & CHORUS
"The Gods on Tap" .... DELORES, JUPITER, MERCURY & CHORUS
"Surprise!" .... SOSIA
"Love—What a Concept" .... JUPITER & MERCURY
"Wait 'Til It Dawns" .... MERCURY
"I Know My Wife" .... AMPHITRYON
"It Was Me" .... SOSIA
"Back So Soon?" .... AMPHITRYON, SOSIA & CHORUS
"Wonderful" .... ALCMENE
"At Liberty in Thebes" .... CHARIS & CHORUS
"Jupiter Slept Here" .... ENTIRE COMPANY

ACT II

"Back to the Play" .... CHORUS
"Something of Yourself (Don't Bring Her Flowers)" .... MERCURY
"Generals' Pandemonium" .... AMPHITRYON, JUPITER, SOSIA & CHORUS
"Heaven on Earth" (Reprise) .... SOSIA & CHARIS
"Olympus Is a Lonely Town" .... JUPITER
"A Star Is Born" .... DELORES & COMPANY
"Final Sequence" .... AMPHITRYON, ALCMENE, MERCURY, JUPITER,
                                              CHARIS, SOSIA & CHORUS
"Heaven on Earth" (Finale) .... JUPITER & ALCMENE

8

DRAMATIS PERSONAE

JUPITER (a/k/a JOVE)* — A greek god in the first flush of eternal middle age. JUPITER has the makings of a great deity, but has not yet fulfilled his potential. He can be childish, stubborn and selfish — but we must always sense his inherent goodness. Strong high baritone. (SEE NOTE)

MERCURY — Wingfooted messenger of the gods, in his early twenties, JUPITER's son and cohort. While he enjoys making mischief, MERCURY has an unspoken agenda: he wants to see JUPITER realize his potential as a great god of love and compassion. JUPITER and MERCURY's father/son relationship is key to the play, even though most of the time MERCURY acts as the parent and JUPITER seems like the child. Lyric baritone.

GENERAL AMPHITRYON* — Commander-in-Chief of Thebes, a military man in his prime. AMPHITRYON first appears as the classic braggart soldier, but in the end proves himself to be a true hero, capable of enormous self-sacrifice. Strong high baritone. (SEE NOTE)

ALCMENE — A beautiful, sensuous woman in her twenties, wife to GENERAL AMPHITRYON. ALCMENE is a woman who enjoys her relationship with her husband and values her reputation. As the play unfolds, she reveals touches of being a contemporary "princess," but always maintains her dignity. Soprano.

SOSIA — A woebegone middle-aged servant, slave to GENERAL AMPHITRYON. SOSIA is intended as a role for a clown, someone capable of casting a cynically humorous eye at the insane world he inhabits. Baritone character voice.

CHARIS — A shrewish, middle-aged servant, slave to PRINCESS ALCMENE. CHARIS purports to be a woman of great dignity and high moral character, but she is actually quite common, and seethes with secret lust. Strong alto belt.

------

*NOTE — The roles of JUPITER and AMPHITRYON *must* be played by the same actor.

9

The Chorus:

Tom, Dick & Horace — The three men of The Chorus are good singer/dancers with a strong sense of comedy. They double as Citizens of Thebes, Household Slaves, and Theban Generals.

Tom is tall and has a beard, Dick is bookish and wears glasses, Horace is short, hip and black. The actor playing Tom also plays the "Amphitryon" double, and must be of the same physical stature as the actor playing the dual roles of Jupiter and Amphitryon.

If the director elects to use additional men in The Chorus, each should have some distinguishing characteristic — a moustache, baldness, etc.

Delores — Delores is an adorably dizzy, curvaceous redhead in her late twenties. Though listed as a member of The Chorus, she is really the leading lady of the play.

This is her story: she met and married Murray The Furrier, the play's fictional producer, while she was appearing as a topless dancer in a Lake Tahoe revue. She has convinced her new husband to back the play, with the understanding that she gets a part in The Chorus.

The unspoken joke of the play is that all of Delores's numbers have been inserted at her and Murray's insistence, much to the chagrin of the other actors. The players are thus forced to suffer through her songs, and even offer backup support in her big number in Act Two, "A Star Is Born." In addition, Delores designed her own tacky costumes, which are at odds with the rest of the play, and which always feature one of Murray's furs.

Care should be taken that Delores is not played as too knowingly ambitious or too campily bitchy. The opposite is true; she should come across as a lovable, vastly untalented clutz who simply adores being on stage. She always speaks directly and honestly to the audience, except in the final High Priest-

ESS scene, where she is very busy acting (horribly). And she always, always displays MURRAY's ratty furs with enormous pride.

* * *

PRONUNCIATION GUIDE

<table>
<tr><td>Amphitryon</td><td>(Am-FIT-tree-on)</td></tr>
<tr><td>Alcmene</td><td>(Alk-MEE-nee)</td></tr>
<tr><td>Sosia</td><td>(SO-see-ah)</td></tr>
<tr><td>Charis</td><td>(KÂR-iss)</td></tr>
<tr><td>Thebes</td><td>(THEEBZ)</td></tr>
<tr><td>Leda</td><td>(LEE-duh)</td></tr>
<tr><td>Jove</td><td>(Rhymes with STOVE)</td></tr>
</table>

FINAL RUNNING ORDER

MUSICAL NUMBERS

ACT I

"Welcome to Greece" . . . . Chorus
"Heaven on Earth" . . . . Jupiter, Alcmene & Chorus
"The Gods on Tap" . . . . Delores, Jupiter, Mercury & Chorus
"Surprise!" . . . . Sosia
"Love — What a Concept" . . . . Jupiter & Mercury
"Wait 'Til It Dawns" . . . . Mercury
"I Know My Wife" . . . . Amphitryon
"It Was Me" . . . . Sosia
"Back So Soon?" . . . . Amphitryon, Sosia & Chorus
"Wonderful" . . . . Alcmene
"At Liberty in Thebes" . . . . Charis & Chorus
"Jupiter Slept Here" . . . . Entire Company

ACT II

"Back to the Play" . . . . Chorus
"Something of Yourself
   (Don't Bring Her Flowers)" . . . . Mercury
"Generals' Pandemonium" . . . . Amphitryon, Jupiter,
Sosia & Chorus
"Heaven on Earth" (Reprise) . . . . Sosia & Charis
"Olympus Is a Lonely Town" . . . . Jupiter
"A Star Is Born" . . . . Delores & Company
"Final Sequence" . . . . Amphitryon, Alcmene, Mercury,
Jupiter, Charis, Sosia & Chorus
"Heaven on Earth" (Finale) . . . . Jupiter & Alcmene

The play is set in the ancient Greek city of Thebes, during the course of a 41-hour day.

Olympus on My Mind

ACT ONE

*The action takes place in the city of Thebes, before the palace of GENERAL AMPHITRYON. Exits downstage left and right, and exits upstage to the garden (*S.R.*) and palace (*S.L.*).*

[MUSIC #1 — WELCOME TO GREECE]

The lights dim and the members of THE CHORUS enter, in a stately fashion. All are dressed in classical garb. TOM is tall, bearded and patrician in appearance. DICK is bookish, of medium height and wears glasses. HORACE is short, hip and black.

The somber mood is broken by the sudden appearance of DE-LORES, a delicious red-headed chorine. She wears a skimpy Grecian showgirl costume, and carries a fur muff.

DELORES. (*shouted*) Hello!

THE CHORUS. (*sings*)
WELCOME TO GREECE!
WELCOME TO GREECE!
GREECE IS THE SETTING OF OUR PIECE!

WE ARE THE CHORUS!
  TOM.
TOM . . .
  DICK.
DICK . . .
  HORACE.
AND HORACE!
  DELORES.
MY NAME'S DELORES!
  THE CHORUS.
WELCOME TO GREECE!

THIS IS A MYTH,
AN ANCIENT MYTH.
BET YOU'VE NEVER SEEN AN ANCIENT MYTH —
LIKE THITH!

WE ARE THE CHORUS.
PLEASE DON'T IGNORE US.
　Delores.
MY NAME'S DELORES!
　The Chorus.
WELCOME TO GREECE!

(*DELORES "hides" behind the three men.*)

　Tom, Dick and Horace.
AT FIRST, THERE WERE JUST THREE OF US . . .
HIM AND HIM AND ME.
　Tom.
TOM . . .
　Dick.
AND DICK . . .
　Horace.
AND HORACE . . .
　Tom, Dick and Horace.
HAPPY AS CAN BE!

(*In showgirl fashion, DELORES struts forward.*)

　Tom, Dick and Horace. (*continued*)
SUDDENLY, THERE'S FOUR OF US!
HOW DID OUR GARDEN GROW?
WHY DID THEY ADD ONE MORE OF US?
　Delores. (*horribly off-key*)
MY HUSBAND BACKED THE SHOW!
　Tom, Dick and Horace.
HER HUSBAND BACKED THE SHOW!
　Tom, Dick and Horace.
WELCOME DELORES
INTO THE CHORUS!
(*spoken*) Do something for us, Delores!

(*DELORES performs her signature routine — a series of poses
　　accompanied by squeals, in which she proudly displays her
　　ample physical attributes.*)

　Delores.
WELCOME!

Tom, Dick and Horace.
WELCOME!
The Chorus.
WELCOME . . .
WELCOME TO GREECE!
Delores. (*shouted*) Hello!

[MUSIC #1A — HEAVENLY CHORDS]

(*The applause is broken by three loud, majestic chords.*)

(*The men form a diagonal stage right, and DELORES moves stage left. "Old" JUPITER is revealed upstage center, behind a scrim, poised against a starry sky. He sports a gray beard and long, flowing robes.*)

(*THE CHORUS addresses us directly, in declamatory fashion.*)

The Chorus. Jupiter! Greatest of the Olympian gods! All-seeing . . . all-knowing . . . all wise.
Tom. Renowned for his infinite goodness, and . . .
The Chorus. His eternal compassion.
Delores. His eternal compassion! (*stepping forward, explaining*) Which is why I told my husband—Murray the Furrier—to invest. "Murray," I said, "this Jupiter is one nice god."
Tom, Dick and Horace. But such was not always the case!
Dick. There was a time when Jupiter was heartless and unfeeling!
Horace. Selfish and uncaring!
Tom. A time when almighty God was . . .
Tom, Dick and Horace. Godawful.
Delores. Godawful. Ptooey. "Oh, but don't worry, Murray," I said. "He comes out okay in the end. And with a couple of new numbers, I bet we can make this one heckuva show!"

(*Lights dim on "Old" JUPITER.*)

Tom, Dick and Horace. (*moving forward*) What made Jupiter reform? What cataclysmic event brought about his miraculous transformation? Tonight, we bring you that story!
Delores. That story!

[MUSIC #1B—WELCOME TO GREECE PLAYOFF]

THE CHORUS. (*sings*)
WELCOME TO GREECE!
WELCOME TO GREECE!
HERE ANCIENT WONDERS NEVER CEASE.

WE ARE THE CHORUS . . .
TOM, DICK AND HORACE.
  DELORES.
MY NAME'S DELORES!
  THE CHORUS. (*exiting*)
WELCOME TO—

(*JUPITER rushes in, now dressed in the garb of a military general, but with a wreath on his head. He is tall and dashing, in the first flush of eternal middle age, and very happy to be here.*)

JUPITER. Greece! Greece at last, and the city of Thebes! And the palace of Amphitryon! Oh, it's good to be back on earth. I've had Olympus on my mind far too long.

(*MERCURY, winged messenger of the gods, enters. He wears the garb of a slave, and is carrying a sword.*)

MERCURY. Father! Will you please slow down? The wings on my heels are killing me.
  JUPITER. Mercury! Forgive me, my son. I couldn't help dashing ahead. I tremble with anticipation!
  MERCURY. There is much to be done. Tremble later.
  JUPITER. Do you know, I believe this will be my most inspired disguise. I've never acted like a human being before.
  MERCURY. And never will again, I warrant. You don't know what you're letting yourself in for. Mortals have a host of emotions you know nothing about.
  JUPITER. Emotions? What are emotions?
  MERCURY. Don't worry. You'll find out soon enough. (*He hands JUPITER the sword.*)
  JUPITER. Oh, goody. I like surprises! Now remember, Mercury. From here on in, you are to refer to me as General Amphitryon, Commander-in-Chief of Thebes. And I shall refer to you as Sosia, my loyal slave!

MERCURY. Really, Father. I wish you'd reconsider. Conniving your way into a woman's arms by impersonating her husband . . . it's so undignified.

JUPITER. Please, Mercury. Don't start that again. Even the Creator of the Universe deserves a day off now and then.

MERCURY. But think of the lady. She may not approve of your intentions.

JUPITER. Nonsense. What more could a woman desire than the divine rapture . . . the celestial euphoria . . . the empyrean ecstasy of a night in bed with me? (*He trips.*)

[MUSIC #1C — SENNETS]

(*Offstage trumpeters, heralding someone's arrival, are heard.*)

JUPITER. (*continued*) That must be her! Quickly, hide! (*JUPITER and MERCURY move right, hiding behind a column.*) Here she comes. My conquest for the night!

[MUSIC #1D — ENTER CHARIS]

(*MUSIC accompanies CHARIS, as she enters from the palace. She is a middle-aged shrew, servant to the princess and a terror to behold. She comes down center, and scans the horizon.*)

MERCURY. We came all the way from heaven . . . for that?

JUPITER. Not her, you idiot. That's Charis, the chief handmaiden. (*CHARIS blows her nose, loudly.*) She's your wife.

MERCURY. My wife? You never told me I was married!

JUPITER. Didn't I? Must've slipped my mind. Look!

[MUSIC #1E — ENTER ALCMENE]

(*MUSIC accompanies ALCMENE, as she enters from the palace. She is a demure, beautiful woman in her twenties. She freezes, as:*)

JUPITER. (*continued*) Isn't she ravishing?

MERCURY. Beautiful. What's her name?

JUPITER. Alcmene. The princess Alcmene!

(*MUSIC accompanies ALCMENE as she moves downstage, joining CHARIS.*)

ALCMENE. Any sign, Charis dear?

CHARIS. None, my lady. None at all.

ALCMENE. None? And today marks a year since our husbands departed for the wars. Oh, Charis, what are we to do? Our men may never return. Perhaps they are already—

CHARIS. Hush, my lady! We mustn't even think such things! (*She makes a sign to ward off evil spirits, and spits three times.*) Never fear. As sure as I am a virtuous woman, the master shall return home victorious, with a king's ransom for his young bride.

ALCMENE. I don't want a king's ransom. All I'll ever want or need in this life is my husband Amphitryon.

JUPITER. (*sotto voce*) Mercury, tell my brother Apollo to hold back the dawn. It's going to be a long night.

MERCURY. Father, wait. This will never work. You haven't the faintest idea of how mortals behave.

JUPITER. Oh, no? Watch this. (*moves forward, presenting himself*) Oh, honey. I'm home!

[MUSIC #1F — HONEY, I'M HOME]

ALCMENE. . . . Amphitryon!

CHARIS. My lord!

ALCMENE. And Sosia!

CHARIS. My husband!

ALCMENE. I can hardly believe my eyes.

MERCURY. (*staring at CHARIS*) Me neither.

ALCMENE. Oh, darling. Is it really you? (*MUSIC out.*)

JUPITER. Funny you should say that. Come, kiss me and see for yourself!

(*JUPITER takes ALCMENE in his arms and they kiss.*)

[MUSIC #1G — HEAVENLY CHORDS II]

(*During the kiss, the three majestic chords are heard again, accompanied by lightning and thunder. ALCMENE backs away, frightened.*)

JUPITER. (*continued*) My sweet! Is something the matter?

ALCMENE. I . . . I don't know. Is it because we've been apart for so long? Just as we kissed, I felt a strange and ominous sense of foreboding.

JUPITER. Foreboding? (*laughs*) No. Anticipation!

[MUSIC #2—HEAVEN ON EARTH]

JUPITER. (*continued*) Of the glorious night that lies before us! (*sings*)
LADY . . . LADY . . .
LAY YOUR FEARS TO REST.
NO NEED TO BE APPREHENSIVE—
LAY YOUR HEAD UPON MY CHEST.
LADY . . . LADY . . .
PUT YOUR TRUST IN ME.
I CAN GUARANTEE
TONIGHT WILL BE . . .

HEAVEN ON EARTH!
HEAVEN ON EARTH!
WE WILL TAKE TO THE SKY.
WE WILL FLY, YOU AND I.
WE WILL LEAVE THIS WORLD BEHIND.
HERE IN MY ARMS YOU'LL FIND
HEAVEN ON EARTH!
HEAVEN ON EARTH!

ALCMENE. (*sings*)
TOUCH ME . . . TOUCH ME . . .
AND I'M NOT AFRAID.
SOMEHOW WHEN YOUR ARMS ENFOLD ME,
ALL MY INHIBITIONS FADE.
FUNNY . . . FUNNY . . .
WHAT CAME OVER ME?
WHY WAS I FRIGHTENED?
WHAT WAS I SCARED OF?
ANY NIGHT WITH YOU WOULD BE . . .

(*The CHORUS sings backup from offstage.*)
HEAVEN ON EARTH!
HEAVEN ON EARTH!
LIKE A STAR UP ON HIGH,
WE WILL SHINE, YOU AND I,
WITH OUR HEARTS AND SOULS ENTWINED.
JUPITER and ALCMENE.
FIRE AND ICE COMBINED!
ALCMENE.
HEAVEN ON EARTH . . .

JUPITER.
I WILL TAKE YOU PLACES
YOU HAVE NEVER BEEN BEFORE. . . .
ALCMENE.
WHY SHOULD I HAVE FELT AFRAID,
WHEN YOUR TOUCH FEELS SO RIGHT?
JUPITER.
I WILL SHOW YOU WONDERS,
GIVE YOU NEW WORLDS TO EXPLORE . . .
ALCMENE.
WHEN WE KISSED, MY SOUL TOOK FLIGHT!
JUPITER and ALCMENE.
TOGETHER WE WILL MAKE TONIGHT . . .

HEAVEN ON EARTH!
HEAVEN ON EARTH!
WE WILL TAKE TO THE SKY.
WE WILL FLY, YOU AND I.
WE WILL LEAVE THIS WORLD BEHIND . . .
JUPITER.
DEEP IN THE NIGHT WE'LL FIND . . .
JUPITER and ALCMENE.
BODIES AND SOULS ENTWINED.

(*JUPITER and ALCMENE kiss.*)

HEAVEN ON EARTH!

(*Applause.*)

ALCMENE. Charis, prepare the bedchambers. At once.

[MUSIC #2A — HEAVEN ON EARTH — PLAYOFF]

CHARIS. (*calling offstage*) Prepare the bedchambers!
OFFSTAGE VOICES. Prepare the bedchambers, prepare the bed-
chambers!
CHARIS. (*turning to MERCURY*) Sosia!

(*She runs into MERCURY's arms, nearly knocking him over.*)

JUPITER. (*embracing ALCMENE*) Oh, it's good to be home.
Right, "Sosia?"

MERCURY. (*locked in CHARIS's embrace*) Sire, may I speak to you a moment? Alone?

ALCMENE. Go ahead, darling. We need a little time to prepare. (*turning to CHARIS*) Charis, they're home. Our husbands are finally home!

(*The women exit, CHARIS tossing a kiss to MERCURY. MUSIC out.*)

MERCURY. This is the limit. I refuse to go through with it!

JUPITER. Please, Mercury? For me? I'm having such fun.

MERCURY. But we'll never carry this off. We are gods. No one is ever going to believe that we are—

(*TOM, DICK and HORACE enter, dressed as CITIZENS OF THEBES.*)

TOM. Amphitryon!

DICK. And Sosia!

HORACE. Can it be? You've returned?

JUPITER. Looks that way, doesn't it?

TOM. Then the rumors are true?

DICK. The Spartans have been defeated?

HORACE. Citizens of Thebes, praise be to Jupiter!

TOM and DICK. Praise be to Jupiter!

JUPITER. Why, thank you. (*MERCURY pokes JUPITER.*)

TOM. General, we've had so little news. Won't you give us a full report?

JUPITER. Report? Report on what?

TOM. Why, the wars!

TOM and DICK. Your battles!

TOM, DICK and HORACE. Everything!

MERCURY. Yes, "General." Why don't you tell them? How did you win the war?

JUPITER. How did I win the war? (*sotto voce, to MERCURY*) . . . How *did* I win the war?

[MUSIC #3 — THE GODS ON TAP]

(*DELORES runs on, wearing a pillbox fur hat and, a matching fox stole.*)

DELORES. (*winking*) I know! (*sings*)
WHY WAS WINNING SUCH A SNAP?
HOW DID WE WIPE THEM OFF THE MAP?
WHAT BROUGHT US VICTORY
AGAINST OUR ENEMY?
WE HAD THE GODS ON . . .
(*dancing to center stage*)
1—2—3—4—5—6—TAP!

ONCE THEY CAUGHT US IN A TRAP . . .
   TOM, DICK and HORACE.
ONCE THEY CAUGHT US IN A TRAP!
   DELORES.
HOW DID OUR ARMY CLOSE THE GAP?
   TOM, DICK and HORACE.
HOW DID OUR ARMY CLOSE THE GAP?
   DELORES.
WHY DID THE SPARTANS LOSE?
HAVEN'T YOU HEARD THE NEWS?
   THE CHORUS.
WE HAD THE GODS ON TAP!
   DELORES.
BECAUSE THE DEITIES
WERE ON OUR SIDE,
WE BROUGHT THEM TO THEIR KNEES
AND TURNED THE TIDE.
WITHOUT THOSE DEITIES
THEY WOULD HAVE DIED!
   TOM, DICK and HORACE.
NO!
   JUPITER and MERCURY.
YES!
WITHOUT HEAVEN'S BACKING,
WE'D HAVE HAD A GOOD SHELLACKING!

   DELORES, JUPITER and MERCURY.
SPARTA HAD A HANDICAP . . .
   TOM, DICK and HORACE.
SPARTA HAD A HANDICAP!
   DELORES.
THAT'S WHY THEY MET WITH SUCH MISHAP!
   TOM, DICK and HORACE.
THAT'S WHY THEY MET WITH SUCH MISHAP!

Jupiter and Mercury.
THEY NEVER HAD A CHANCE
OF STOPPING OUR ADVANCE.
    Delores and All.
WE HAD THE GODS ON . . .

(*JUPITER and MERCURY watch as DELORES and THE CIT-
IZENS OF THEBES perform. A slow soft-shoe section is
followed by a fast routine. The men execute a legitimate
combination, while DELORES gamely demonstrates her
nodding acquaintance with rudimentary tap. At the end, she
rushes into place for a final pose.*)

    Delores.
TAP!

(*Applause. DELORES signals conductor, and:*)

[MUSIC #3A — THE GODS ON TAP PLAYOFF]

    Delores.
HEAVEN PUT IT IN OUR LAP . . .
    All.
HEAVEN PUT IT IN OUR LAP . . .
    Delores.
WITH ONE GIGANTIC THUNDERCLAP!
    All.
ONE BIG GIGANTIC THUNDERCLAP!
    Delores.
THE SPARTANS TURNED AND LOOKED—
THEY KNEW THEIR GOOSE WAS COOKED.
    Delores and All.
WE HAD THE GODS ON . . .

(*ALCMENE and CHARIS emerge from the palace. THE CHO-
RUS continues to tap in place.*)

    Alcmene. Amphitryon!
    Charis. Sosia!
    Mercury. (*seeing CHARIS and starting off*) . . . Oh, no.
No way.

(*JUPITER grabs him and the gods exit into the palace, with the
two women.*)

Tom, Dick and Horace. (*exiting*)
WE HAD THE GODS ON . . .
Delores. (*remaining on stage*)
TAP!!!

(*After the applause:*)

[MUSIC #3B — THE STORM]

(*MUSIC accompanies much lightning and thunder.*)

Delores. Seventeen hours go by! All night, a fierce storm rages! Enter . . . Sosia, the slave.

(*MUSIC segues directly into:*)

[MUSIC #3C — ENTER SOSIA — EXIT DELORES]

(*SOSIA, a middle-aged, woebegone slave, enters. He is dressed in the same garb as MERCURY.*)

Sosia. Home! Home at last!
Delores. (*interrupting SOSIA*) Break a leg, cutie!

(*MUSIC accompanies DELORES as she taps off. SOSIA gives the audience a look, and exits. He re-enters, starting the scene anew.*)

Sosia. Home! Home at last, after a year of war! Oh, thank you, merciful gods . . . Then again, if you are so merciful, why did you make me a slave? (*addressing us directly*)
I wanna tell ya. This is no life for a human being. Sent out in this storm, just to bring home a message to my master's wife? Big deal, so we won the war. The news couldn't keep til morning? (*shrugs*)
Anyway, I'm home. And now for something to eat. I wanna tell ya . . . I am so hungry, I could eat a Trojan horse.

(*He starts to exit, just as MERCURY emerges from the palace.*)

Sosia. Hi.
Mercury. Hi yourself.

(*The two doubles stop dead in their tracks, and turn. They rush
    up to inspect each other. After a moment:*)

SOSIA. I gotta stop drinking this cheap Spartan wine. I look
terrible. (*He starts into palace. MERCURY blocks his way.*)
    MERCURY. Wait a second. You can't go in there.
    SOSIA. No? And why not?
    MERCURY. Why not? Because. This is the house of General
Amphitryon.
    SOSIA. I know that! I am Sosia, slave to Amphitryon.
    MERCURY. Sosia? Did you say, "Sosia?" Liar, liar, pants on
fire!
    SOSIA. But I *am* Sosia! Ask anyone! Can I deny what I know
to be true? Deny the name my parents gave me? Can a man deny
his very existence? Don't answer, these are rhetorical questions.
No, by the gods, I swear *I* am Sosia!

(*MERCURY makes a gesture with his hand, and SOSIA reacts
    as if he has been "zapped." Each "zap" is a sound cue.*)

[MUSIC #3D — FIRST "ZAP"]

SOSIA. (*continued*) Then again, I could be wrong.
    MERCURY. I knew you lied, vermin. For in truth, *I* am Sosia.
    SOSIA. You . . . are Sosia?
    MERCURY. And let he who challenges me, beware my . . . (*pro-
ducing a short branch*) . . . stick.
    SOSIA. And a lovely stick it is. (*to himself*) He's got to be crazy!
(*back to MERCURY*) Listen, Chuckles . . . If you are Sosia,
then you know everything Sosia knows, right?
    MERCURY. Right.
    SOSIA. Then tell me, "Sosia." Where were you during our final
battle with the Spartans?
    MERCURY. Let's see. Where would Sosia be? Hiding in my
master's tent, getting drunk?
    SOSIA. (*to himself*) He knows! But how could he? Unless he
really is . . . (*to MERCURY*) And if you are, who does that
make me?
    MERCURY. What's it matter? You were a nothing to begin with.
    SOSIA. (*starting to cry*) But now I'm no one to speak of at all!
(*He cries in a high falsetto.*)
    MERCURY. Quiet down. Lower your voice! (*SOSIA continues

to cry, in a lower register.) All right. If it means that much to you, when I am through being Sosia, you can resume the job. (*MUSIC.*)

[MUSIC #4 — SURPRISE!]

SOSIA. This is only temporary?
MERCURY. (*starting to exit*) You think I enjoy being a lowlife? (*MUSIC.*)
SOSIA. I don't believe this is happening . . . Wait! You can't be serious! Who put you up to this? . . . Wait a second. Wait a second! Is this a surprise party? (*Song intro begins.*) Aw, you shouldn't have! (*sings*)
DON'T TELL ME. DON'T TELL ME.
THE WHOLE THING IS A HOAX, RIGHT?
JUST ONE OF THOSE SILLY JOKES, RIGHT?
AND I'M THE BUTT—
YOU CRAZY NUT.

YOU'RE KIDDING. DON'T TELL ME.
I WALKED INTO A SET-UP,
WITH YOU IN THIS CORNY GET-UP.
I'M SO NAIVE,
I CAN'T BELIEVE
THE WAY YOU HAD ME GOING—
I FELL FOR IT HOOK, LINE AND SINKER.
I HAD NO WAY OF KNOWING . . .
I THOUGHT THAT YOU WERE SERIOUS,
YOU DIRTY LITTLE STINKER!
(*He looks around, nervously. Spoken:*) Okay, so where is every-one?
MERCURY. No one else is coming.
SOSIA. Oh, I get it. One of those small, intimate parties. Listen, I hate to be rude after you've gone to all this trouble, but I am just pooped. These late night hikes, know what I mean? (*sings*)

FORGIVE ME FOR YAWNING.
IT REALLY WAS TO LAUGH, KID.
A CARNIVAL AND A HALF, KID.
IT'S ALL BEEN FUN,
NO HARM'S BEEN DONE,
BUT NOW I'VE REALLY GOT TO RUN.
FORGIVE ME, BUT I MUST BE ON MY WAY.

AND THANKS A BUNCH . . .
YOU REALLY MADE MY DAY!

(*MUSIC continues as he starts into palace. MERCURY zaps
him repeatedly, and pulls him back into courtyard, away
from the palace door. MERCURY exits.*)

SOSIA. (*continued; dizzy*) Hey. What kind of party is this?
. . . Wait a second. I get it. (*sings*)

I'M DREAMING. I MUST BE.
AND NONE OF THIS IS REAL, RIGHT?
I KNEW IT JUST DIDN'T FEEL RIGHT.
IT'S ALL A FAKE.
I'LL SOON AWAKE
AND FIND IT'S JUST A BIG MISTAKE.
YES, SUDDENLY THE WHOLE THING'S VERY CLEAR.
I'LL RUB MY EYES . . .
AND YOU'LL JUST DISAPPEAR!
(*SOSIA starts into palace, but is greeted by MERCURY. Spoken:*)
. . . Still here?
MERCURY. Surprise!

(*Applause. MERCURY starts to advance on SOSIA.*)

SOSIA. Okay, tell you what I'm gonna do. Since you're so in-
tent on being me, I will gladly lease you the privilege.
MERCURY. Lease?
SOSIA. For shall we say, three gold pieces?
MERCURY. Three gold pieces?
SOSIA. Reasonable, don't you think? Of course, if you want to
throw in a large sack of wine . . .
MERCURY. Three gold pieces and a large sack of wine?
SOSIA. You're right. I'm not worth that much. Make it a small
sack. (*MERCURY zaps him.*)

[MUSIC #4A — ZAPS II]

SOSIA. (*continued*) You drive a hard bargain. Two gold pieces,
and forget the wine. (*MERCURY zaps him again.*) You've got a
better idea?
MERCURY. Why don't I break every bone in your body, then
feed you to the dogs? (*He gives SOSIA a final zap, pushing him
to ground.*)

Sosia. All right, I'm going! Just trying to earn an honest drachma. Well, this is goodbye. I'll see me later. Don't do anything *I* wouldn't do. Take good care of myself! (*He exits, laughing like a madman. He runs back on, addressing the audience:*) My master! How do I explain this to my master? . . . Why am I asking *you*?

(*SOSIA exits.*)

[MUSIC #4B — SENNETS II]

Mercury. Silly mortal left just in time. After seventeen hours with the princess, Father is taking his leave.

[MUSIC #4C — HARD NIGHT]

(*JUPITER staggers out of the palace, holding a flower. He stares into space, dreamily.*)

Mercury. (*continued*) Father, are you all right?
Jupiter. No, I'm not. Something happened in there last night. I made a discovery. A miraculous new discovery!
Mercury. Why Father, how clever of you. And what do we call this new discovery?
Jupiter. I don't know. I haven't named it yet. But it's this wonderful feeling I get, every time I gaze at or even think of the princess!
Mercury. Father, that's nothing new. It's a human emotion, called "love." Mortals have known about it for centuries.
Jupiter. Don't be absurd. No one has ever felt this way before. This is a wholly original, never-before-experienced . . . what did you call it?
Mercury. Love.
Jupiter. Love?

[MUSIC #5 — "LOVE — WHAT A CONCEPT"]

Mercury. Love.
Jupiter. Love . . . What a concept! (*sings*)
LOVE — WHAT A CONCEPT!
LOVE — WHAT A NOTION!
LOVE MAY BE THE GREATEST INVENTION
SINCE MANKIND WAS FIRST — PAY ATTENTION!

LOVE – WHY, IT'S BRILLIANT!
LOVE . . .
   MERCURY. (*helpfully*)
AN EMOTION.
   JUPITER.
UNLIKE ANY OTHER I'VE KNOWN . . .
   MERCURY.
LOVE . . .
   JUPITER.
HAS PROPERTIES ALL ITS OWN!

   JUPITER and MERCURY.
LO-O-O-O-O-O-OVE
   JUPITER.
PACKS THE WALLOP OF A . . .
   MERCURY.
BOLT OUT OF THE BLUE!
   JUPITER.
TRY TO RESIST IT . . .
   MERCURY.
YOU'RE UNABLE.
   JUPITER and MERCURY.
LOVE LOVE LOVE LOVE LOVE LOVE LOVE
   JUPITER.
HAS A DOLLOP OF THE . . .
   MERCURY.
WILD!
   JUPITER.
AND . . .
   MERCURY.
STRANGE!
   JUPITER.
AND . . .
   MERCURY.
NEW!
   JUPITER.
HARD TO DEFINE . . .
   JUPITER and MERCURY.
BUT EASY TO LABEL!

LOVE – WHAT A CONCEPT!

Mercury.
GOSH, WHAT A BRAINSTORM!
Jupiter.
I WOKE UP THIS MORNING TO FIND
SOMETHING NEW HAD ENTERED MY MIND.
Jupiter and Mercury.
WHO'D HAVE THOUGHT IT COULD BE?
Mercury.
LOVE . . .
Jupiter.
HAS SUDDENLY DAWNED ON ME!

(*JUPITER leaps about, excitedly.*)

Mercury. Father, I've never seen you like this before!
Jupiter. I know. Don't you love it!?
Mercury. But what of the princess? Is she equally in love?
Jupiter. Do you think it possible? Could she feel the same for me as I do her?
Mercury. Of course it's possible. That's what love is all about!

Jupiter.
LOVE—WHAT A CONCEPT!
Mercury.
GOD, YOU'RE A GENIUS!
Jupiter.
STRONG ENOUGH TO DRIVE YOU INSANE,
LOVE HAS TAKEN HOLD IN MY BRAIN.
Jupiter and Mercury.
HEAVEN IS SMILING ABOVE . . .
Jupiter.
NOW THAT I HAVE DISCOVERED—

(*DELORES enters in toe shoes, tutu and white fox stole, wobbling en pointe. Acting as Cupid, she mimes shooting JUPITER with an arrow.*)

Jupiter, Mercury and Delores.
LOVE!

(*Applause. DELORES wobbles off.*)

Mercury. Well? What did she say? Tell me everything!

JUPITER. There's not much to tell. All she did was murmur "Amphitryon, Amphitryon" all night long.

MERCURY. That's it? No indication she knew of your true identity?

JUPITER. No, not as I recall . . . By thunder! You think she actually fell for this disguise . . . completely?

MERCURY. Certainly sounds that way.

JUPITER. But that's unheard of! They always guess the truth, the moment we're in bed. In the bedchambers, I am unmistakably divine!

[MUSIC #5A — SENNETS III]

MERCURY. The princess!

JUPITER. Good. Now we'll get to the bottom of this!

[MUSIC #5B — ENTER ALCMENE II]

(*ALCMENE enters from the palace.*)

ALCMENE. My lord. Are you leaving, so soon?

JUPITER. Forgive me, my pet. But you know how it is. The sun won't shine, til I give the orders.

ALCMENE. (*smiling*) Darling, you take yourself entirely too seriously. You think the world can't get along without you?

JUPITER. Not for long. Dearest, before I leave, there is one matter I must bring before you. Something of great importance to me.

ALCMENE. Yes, darling?

JUPITER. Alcmene, did anything last night strike you as peculiar?

ALCMENE. Peculiar?

JUPITER. Out of the ordinary.

ALCMENE. No, not as I recall.

JUPITER. You're quite sure? Think about it. Did anything about me or my performance strike you as—

ALCMENE. Silly man. Is that why you're in a dither? Not to worry! Amphitryon, you were superb.

JUPITER. . . . "Amphitryon!" Then you noticed nothing? After seventeen hours?

ALCMENE. Seventeen hours? Is that how long it was?

JUPITER. Yes!

ALCMENE. No wonder you're upset. So what if it was shorter than usual! Believe me, while it lasted . . .

JUPITER. Into the house, Alcmene! I would not see your "tears" as I depart.

ALCMENE. Is it time to say goodbye? Already?

JUPITER. I'm afraid so. Goodbye.

[MUSIC #6—HEAVEN ON EARTH (REPRISE)]

JUPITER. (*continued, as ALCMENE starts to exit*) Darling? Last night . . . it was good for you?

ALCMENE. Good? No . . . (*sings*)
HEAVEN ON EARTH!
HEAVEN ON EARTH!
SO FULFILLED AND COMPLETE,
SO INEFFABLY SWEET
THAT MY HEART IS STILL AFLAME.
YOU PUT THE GODS TO SHAME
RIGHT HERE ON EARTH!
(*starts to move off, then*) Try and be home for dinner?

(*ALCMENE exits.*)

JUPITER. Did you hear? She hasn't the slightest idea it was me!

MERCURY. What can I say? I am dumbfounded.

JUPITER. I ought to drop a few thunderbolts on her. That'll teach her who to love!

MERCURY. No, Father. I wouldn't do that. Love doesn't quite work that way.

JUPITER. I don't understand it. How could she confuse me with some everyday, ordinary mortal?

MERCURY. I see but two alternatives. Either you were less than your divine self last night—which is impossible, of course . . .

JUPITER. Of course!

MERCURY. Or, perhaps the experience of you was so shattering . . . it has left the princess momentarily stunned.

(*JUPITER ponders this a moment, then grins.*)

JUPITER. Yes! The poor girl was so overwhelmed, she still doesn't know what hit her! Dear child. How can I bring her back to her senses?

MERCURY. Love is a delicate matter, Father. I'm afraid the only thing to do now is . . . wait.

JUPITER. But I don't want to wait. I want her to love me now!

[MUSIC #7 — WAIT 'TIL IT DAWNS]

MERCURY. (*sings*)
WAIT 'TIL IT DAWNS.
WAIT 'TIL THE SUN STARTS TO CLIMB.
LOVE IS DECEPTIVE;
SHE'LL BE MORE RECEPTIVE,
GIVEN A LITTLE MORE TIME.
   JUPITER. Oh, my son. Do you really think so?
   MERCURY.
WAIT FOR THE LIGHT.
WAIT 'TIL SHE'S GREETED THE DAY.
NOW IT IS NIGHT.
WAIT 'TIL HER DREAMS MELT AWAY.
   JUPITER. Yes! Last night, she deluded herself into believing I
was Amphitryon. But in the cold light of day . . .
   MERCURY.
WAIT UNTIL THE MORNING STAR
HAS CHASED AWAY THE MOON.
DAY REVEALS
WHAT NIGHT CONCEALS.
SOON, SHE'LL CHANGE HER TUNE . . .
   JUPITER. Apollo! Apollo, can you hear me? We must get this
day underway!
   MERCURY. (*and* OFFSTAGE CHORUS)
MORNING IS NIGH . . . (MORNING IS NIGH)
NOW ALL SHE NEEDS IS A CHANCE.
BID NIGHT GOODBYE. (GOODBYE! GOODBYE!)
LET HER WAKE UP TO ROMANCE . . .
   JUPITER. (*exiting*) She will love me, Mercury. Before this day
is through, she will love me!

   MERCURY. (*and* OFFSTAGE CHORUS)
LET HER WAKE UP TO ROMANCE!

   CHARIS. (*from off-stage*) Sosia! . . . Sosia!
   MERCURY. Oh, no. "My wife." They are never going to let me
live this down up in heaven.
   CHARIS. So, there he goes. My husband. The man with as much
feeling as a brick. Oh, ye gods! What have I done to deserve such
treatment?

[MUSIC #8 — CHARIS'S LAMENT]

CHARIS. (*continued, sings*)
NOT A SQUEEZE, NOT A HUG
HAVE I GOTTEN FROM THIS LUG.
NOT SO MUCH
AS A TOUCH
SINCE HE RETURNED.
HAS HE TOLD ME HOW HE MISSED ME?
EMBRACED, CARESSED OR KISSED ME?
OH, YE GODS!
NO, YE GODS!
BEHOLD, A WOMAN SPURNED!

MERCURY. Charis. Dumpling . . .

CHARIS. Don't you "dumpling" me. Your first night home after a year of war, and you sleep out here in the yard. I demand an explanation!

MERCURY. And you deserve one. I just didn't know how to break the news.

CHARIS. What news?

MERCURY. Charis, the man you see before you is not the man you married.

CHARIS. And why not?

MERCURY. Why not? Why not . . . The war! Oh, Charis. War is hell. Awful things happen to men . . . in war. (*He crosses his legs.*)

CHARIS. Oh, Sosia. You don't mean. . . ? (*MERCURY nods, painfully.*) Those filthy Spartans! And that's why you didn't come to bed last night?

MERCURY. (*in falsetto*) Uh huh.

CHARIS. If that isn't just like you. Always losing something! My mother was right. I never should have married you.

MERCURY. Well, pardon me. Maybe you should try your luck elsewhere. If you find a taker, you have my blessing. And he, my pity.

CHARIS. Hear how I'm repaid! Twenty years of unstinting devotion. Twenty years, a spotless reputation. And now you'd have me sink to the depths of depravity?

MERCURY. It's a step up.

CHARIS. Wretch! The gods know me for an honorable woman.

MERCURY. The gods hardly know you at all. And what little they do know, they'd like to forget!

CHARIS. Go on, encourage me. You'll be sorry. A whole group of men in this town lust after my body.

MERCURY. Charis, you leave those poor lepers alone!

(*Incensed, CHARIS exits.*)

[MUSIC #9 — ENTER THE HUSBAND]

TOM, DICK and HORACE. (*rushing on, singing*)
ENTER THE HUSBAND!
ENTER THE HUSBAND!
ENTER . . . ENTER . . .
ENTER THE HUSBAND!

(*MERCURY exits.*)

(*GENERAL AMPHITRYON enters. He is dressed identically to JUPITER, save for a military helmet which covers his face. On his arm is DELORES, who sports yet another of her endless fur wraps.*)

TOM, DICK and HORACE. (*continued*)
ENTER THE HUSBAND . . .
DELORES. (*to audience, referring to AMPHITRYON*) Oh no, this isn't Murray!
TOM, DICK and HORACE.
ENTER THE HUSBAND . . .
DELORES. He's married to the prin*cess!*
TOM, DICK and HORACE.
ENTER! ENTER!
ENTER THE HUSBAND!

(*AMPHITRYON removes his helmet, and hands it to DELORES. We now see AMPHITRYON is played by the same actor who plays the role of JUPITER.*)

AMPHITRYON. Home! Home at last, after a year of war. Oh, what a happy day for my beloved wife. Think of her.

[MUSIC #10 — I KNOW MY WIFE]

AMPHITRYON. (*continued*) A whole year, without the one thing that gives her paltry existence any meaning whatsoever.
DELORES. Meaning . . . ?
AMPHITRYON. Meaning . . . me!

(*THE CHORUS salutes and marches off. DELORES leaves the helmet behind.*)

AMPHITRYON. (*continued; sings*)
SHE'S BEEN
SIGHING,
LONELY,
ON HER MIND IS ONE THING ONLY:
HER HUSBAND.
I KNOW MY WIFE.
SHE'S BEEN
CRYING,
PACING,
IN HER NIGHTLY DREAMS EMBRACING
HER HUSBAND.
I KNOW MY WIFE.

EVER SINCE I LEFT
SHE'S BEEN TOTALLY BEREFT,
MOONING ABOUT THE HOUSE.
SHE FILLS HER EMPTY HOURS
DRESSING DOLLS AND PRESSING FLOWERS,
DISCONSOLATE WITHOUT HER SPOUSE—

ALMOST
DYING,
WAITING,
HUNGRILY ANTICIPATING
HER HUSBAND—
LIGHT OF HER LIFE.
SHE'S BEEN HEARTSICK, PINING, LONGING,
  BURNING—
YEARNING FOR HER MATE'S RETURNING.
I KNOW MY WIFE!

I KNOW
THE FIRST THING SHE'LL DO WHEN WE'RE ALONE:
CHECK MY WOUNDS TO SEE IF THEY HAVE FESTERED.
SHE'LL GINGERLY UNDRESS ME,
SOULFULLY CARESS ME . . .
THE REST OF THE NIGHT
IN HER ARMS I'LL BE SEQUESTERED.
THEN, ONCE OUR PASSION HAS BEEN SPENT,
I'LL TELL HER OF THE BATTLES I HAVE FOUGHT.
SHE'LL LISTEN TO ME, EVER SO CONTENT . . .

THEN SHE'LL GAILY DEMAND THE PRESENTS
  I HAVE BROUGHT!

SHE'LL BE
FLYING,
TEASING,
HAPPILY INTENT ON PLEASING
HER HUSBAND—
YOU BET YOUR LIFE!
THERE'S NOT MUCH THAT ONE CAN TAKE AS GIVEN
IN THIS CRAZY WORLD WE LIVE IN,
RIFE WITH WAR AND STRIFE.
BUT I KNOW, I KNOW,
I KNOW MY WIFE!

(*Applause. He looks offstage.*)

AMPHITRYON. (*continued*) Sosia! Sosia, you rascal! Get in here!

SOSIA. (*entering, timidly*) Yes, sire. Please don't beat me again, sire.

AMPHITRYON. Cur! I'll beat you til you've told the truth! Now. Though I long to greet my wife, I shall try to be patient. Tell me your story again . . . from the beginning.

SOSIA. Yes, sire. But shall I tell the truth again? Or shall I act as they do in court, and lie through my teeth?

AMPHITRYON. Sosia, I am waiting. Having received your orders. . . ?

SOSIA. I took the road to Thebes, cursing you and my mission.

AMPHITRYON. What?

SOSIA. You wanted the truth.

AMPHITRYON. And how did your mission proceed?

SOSIA. I put each foot in front of me, leaving my widdle twacks behind.

AMPHITRYON. Spare me the embellishments. Whom did you encounter on the road?

SOSIA. No one. But I was full of fear and horror.

AMPHITRYON. And when you arrived here at home?

SOSIA. Sire, why don't you sit down?

AMPHITRYON. Whom did you meet, Sosia?

SOSIA. Whom did I meet?

AMPHITRYON. You heard the question!

SOSIA. Well, sire . . . it was me.

AMPHITRYON. What are you saying? You met yourself?!
SOSIA. Exactly!

[MUSIC #11 — IT WAS ME]

SOSIA. (*continued, sings*)
IT WAS ME, I, SOSIA . . .
HE WAS STANDING HERE ON GUARD.
ANOTHER ME, ANOTHER I, ANOTHER SOSIA . . .
RIGHT HERE IN OUR YARD.
A "ME" WHO LOOKS JUST LIKE ME —
WE'RE TOTALLY ALIKE FROM HEAD TO TOE.
IT WAS ME, I, SOSIA . . .
THAT NASTY SO-AND-SO.

AMPHITRYON. What sort of lies are these?
SOSIA. The best kind — true lies! Before me, this "I" had arrived on the scene. That is, "I" arrived before *I* got here.
AMPHITRYON. You expect me to believe this?
SOSIA. I don't believe it myself.
AMPHITRYON. To continue: did you go into the house?
SOSIA. Are you crazy? Would "I" allow me to do that? Oh, no! "I" stubbornly refused to allow me to enter!
AMPHITRYON. What? How?
SOSIA. How? With a stick! That famous stick. My back still bears the scars.
AMPHITRYON. So. Someone beat you!
SOSIA. You're telling me.
AMPHITRYON. Well, then. Who in blazes did it?
SOSIA. You're not gonna like it. (*sings*)
IT WAS ME, I, SOSIA . . .
(NOT THE ONE WHO'S STANDING HERE).
THE OTHER ME, THE OTHER I, THE OTHER SOSIA . . .
HAVE I MADE IT CLEAR?
THE "ME" WHO LOOKS JUST LIKE ME —
WHO BEATS LIKE TEN DEMENTED GALLEY SLAVES.
IT WAS ME, I, SOSIA . . .
THAT SCURVIEST OF KNAVES.

AMPHITRYON. Madness! To finish . . . did you see my wife?
SOSIA. No! How could I?
AMPHITRYON. Why? What stopped you?

Sosia. How many times I gotta tell you this? (*sings*)
IT WAS ME, I, SOSIA.
IT WAS ME WHO BARRED THE GATE.
MY BROTHER ME, MY BROTHER I, MY BROTHER
  SOSIA . . .
CAN'T YOU GET THIS STRAIGHT?
THE "ME" WHO LOOKS JUST LIKE ME—
THE ONE WHO STOLE MY SECRETS IS TO BLAME.
IT WAS ME, I, SOSIA . . .
THAT NO GOOD, ROTTEN,
STINGY, MISBEGOTTEN
MISERABLE WHAT'S-HIS-NAME!

(*Applause.*)

Amphitryon. Enough! Cease this drivel! Already you have delayed my reunion with your mistress far too long!

Sosia. Naturally. I am a slave, so it is drivel. Let a nobleman tell this tale, it would be proclaimed a miracle.

Amphitryon. Silence! (*looking offstage*) My wife approaches.

[music #12—back so soon?]

(*He hides behind a pillar, with SOSIA. ALCMENE enters from the palace with CHARIS.*)

Alcmene. No, Charis. Remain here. I go to offer my mid-day devotions.

(*CHARIS curtseys and exits.*)

Amphitryon. Steel yourself, Sosia. For here will be a reunion at which the gods themselves will weep for joy. (*presenting himself*) Alcmene!

Alcmene. . . . Amphitryon! Back so soon?

Amphitryon. (*sings*)
BACK SO SOON?

Sosia.
BACK SO SOON?

Amphitryon.
IS THIS THE WELCOME OF AN ACHING HEART?
"BACK SO SOON,"
DID SHE SAY?

Amphitryon and Sosia.
BACK SO SOON!

Amphitryon.
SHE ACTS AS IF WE'D NEVER BEEN APART!

I FEARED THAT SHE MIGHT TREMBLE,
OR FEEL FAINT AND START TO SWOON.
AT LEAST, SHE'D TELL THE SERVANTS TO ASSEMBLE.
BUT INSTEAD . . .
　Sosia.
BUT INSTEAD . . .
　Amphitryon.
SHE ONLY SAID . . .
　Sosia.
SHE ONLY SAID . . .
　Amphitryon and Sosia.
"BACK SO SOON!"
　Alcmene. Amphitryon, I don't understand . . .

(*THE CHORUS marches on, assuming a variety of Greek tragic
　poses. DELORES wears a fox stole draped over her head.*)

　Amphitryon and Sosia.
BACK SO SOON!
　The Chorus.
BACK SO SOON!
　Amphitryon and Sosia.
BACK SO SOON!
　The Chorus.
BACK SO SOON!
　Amphitryon.
HOW QUICKLY BURNING PASSIONS CAN ABATE!
"BACK SO SOON,"
DID SHE SAY?
　The Chorus.
BACK SO SOON!
　Amphitryon.
AND I HAD WORRIED I WAS COMING LATE!

(*drawing himself up, stiffly*)
FORGIVE IF I'VE INTRUDED,
I'LL RETURN TO MY PLATOON.
IT'S CLEAR THAT FROM YOUR HEART I'VE BEEN
　EXCLUDED.
I THOUGHT, LIKE ME, YOU'D PINED AWAY AND
　BROODED.
I SEE NOW I WAS THOROUGHLY DELUDED.
FOR I APPEAR . . .

SOSIA.
WE APPEAR!
AMPHITRYON.
AFTER A YEAR . . .
THE CHORUS.
AFTER A YEAR!
AMPHITRYON.
ONLY TO HEAR . . .
SOSIA. (*going overboard*)
WHAT DOES HE HEAR?
WHAT DOES HE HEAR?
WHAT DOES HE—?

(*AMPHITRYON and ALCMENE cut him off with a piercing
    look.*)

AMPHITRYON, SOSIA and CHORUS.
BACK SO SOON!!!

(*THE CHORUS exits.*)

ALCMENE. Amphitryon, why do you reproach me? I thought
I paid my debt to you yesterday. If you desire more, I confess I
have no more to give.
AMPHITRYON. Good wife, what are you saying? I appeared to
you yesterday?
ALCMENE. Good husband, what are you asking? As if you did
not remember. As if I could ever forget the beautiful night we
shared.
AMPHITRYON. Alcmene, was it a dream you had, to announce
my coming? Is that why you think you've already satisfied my
love?
ALCMENE. You deny you came here yesterday? That you took
every liberty with me a husband is allowed?
AMPHITRYON. Every liberty a husband—! Sosia, my friend!
Support me!
SOSIA. Shall I fetch a doctor, sire? She could be dangerous.
AMPHITRYON. Alcmene, think of the consequences of what
you say.
ALCMENE. I do not fear the consequences. If you deny you
were here, it makes no matter. My heart knows the truth!
AMPHITRYON. Miserable woman! I suppose you have proof?
ALCMENE. Why would I need proof? As if all the servants did

not see you. Or our dogs rush up to greet you. And what is this? Who gave me this belt? (*She displays the jeweled belt around her waist.*)

AMPHITRYON. You received this belt . . . from me?

ALCMENE. A souvenir of your recent victory. (*pointedly, looking at SOSIA*) Or so I was told.

AMPHITRYON. (*to SOSIA*) Liar! You swore you never saw your mistress last night!

SOSIA. I didn't! The gift belt is right here in the pouch! (*He displays his pouch.*)

AMPHITRYON. My seal is still intact! (*staring at ALCMENE's belt*) And yet, if my eyes do not deceive me . . . Quickly. Open it!

SOSIA. (*opening pouch*) It's gone! The gift belt has vanished!

(*Lightning and thunder.*)

AMPHITRYON. Oh, ye gods! What doom have ye decided for me?

SOSIA. I know! Amphitryon-with-the-Stick got here first—

AMPHITRYON. Silence! Enough of your prattle!

ALCMENE. Well? Do you still insist you did not appear before me?

AMPHITRYON. . . . No. Perhaps I was mistaken. But humor me. Tell me exactly what transpired here last night?

ALCMENE. Amphitryon!

AMPHITRYON. I do not doubt your word. But for reasons of my own, I want to know exactly how it was between us.

ALCMENE. Very well.

[MUSIC #13 — WONDERFUL]

ALCMENE. (*continued, to herself*) Mother told me there'd be days like this. (*sings*)
LAST NIGHT WAS AS EVER, DEAR,
AS IT HAS ALWAYS BEEN.
BUT IF YOU SEEK
A FULL CRITIQUE,
I WILL GLADLY FILL YOU IN.

WONDERFUL . . .
YOU WERE WONDERFUL,
LIKE A GOD FROM ABOVE IN HIS PRIME.
LAST EVENING WAS POETRY—
ESPECIALLY THE FOURTH AND SEVENTEENTH TIME!

BEAUTIFUL . . .
TRULY BEAUTIFUL.
WORDS ALONE CAN'T DESCRIBE HOW I FEEL.
LAST EVENING WAS ECSTASY—
AND THAT THING THAT YOU DID WITH THE STRING
WAS UNREAL.

HOW STRONG YOU WERE!
HOW MASTERFUL!
DASHING AND UNABASHEDLY REGAL.
HOW NICE TO KNOW LOVE CAN BE SO SWEET,
AND STILL COMPLETELY LEGAL.

MARVELOUS!
TOO TOO MARVELOUS!
EVEN NOW IT STILL SEEMS LIKE A DREAM.
LAST EVENING WAS HEAVENLY.
I'M NOT TALKING . . .
(*makes a "so-so" gesture*)
I'M TALKING SUPREME!

FABULOUS! AAAH!
YOU WERE FABULOUS! OOOH!
I COULD HARDLY BELIEVE YOU WERE MINE.
NOTHING SHORT OF WONDERFUL . . .
DARLING, YOU WERE DIVINE!!!

AMPHITRYON. No! No, my deceiving wife, twas not I. Whoever came to you last night was most worthless of vagabonds!

ALCMENE. You still persist?

AMPHITRYON. Please. Leave me my happy memories as they were. Hereafter, I shall seek only to sever our bonds!

ALCMENE. Coward! You lost your heart to another, say so! You want to free yourself of me, I shall grant your wish . . . before nightfall!

AMPHITRYON. Faithless woman! I shall prove *I* was the one deceived! I shall return here with my generals, who will swear I was with them in camp all last night. I shall solve this accursed puzzle, and woe to the man who has deceived me!

SOSIA. Shall I accompany you, sire?

AMPHITRYON. Keep still. Wait here, til I return. Fairy tales! Stuff and nonsense!

(*AMPHITRYON exits.*)

[MUSIC #13A — MARITAL PROBLEMS]

(*MUSIC under, as:*)

ALCMENE. He was here. He gave me this belt. Everyone saw him.

SOSIA. Fret not, my lady. The world is upside down today. All will be resolved when he returns.

(*SOSIA ushers ALCMENE into the garden* USR. *MUSIC out.*)

(*JUPITER and MERCURY enter* DSL.)

JUPITER. You and your big ideas! "Wait til it dawns." She still hasn't the faintest idea I was here.

MERCURY. I misjudged her, father. She's in more of a fog than I realized.

JUPITER. What am I to do? How will I ever win her love?

MERCURY. You could tell her the truth. Reveal yourself.

JUPITER. Now? I'd be too embarrassed.

MERCURY. Well, if you can't tell her directly . . . why not give her a little hint?

JUPITER. Hint? What sort of hint?

MERCURY. Well, remember that gift belt you gave her?

(*MERCURY whispers in his ear. JUPITER giggles.*)

JUPITER. Oh, yes. I like that! Why, it's absolutely inspired!

(*JUPITER and MERCURY exit.*)

(*SOSIA re-enters from garden.*)

SOSIA. Poor master . . . (*He laughs, vindictively.*) Poor mistress . . . (*He leers, suggestively.*) Thank heaven, I can depend on dear old faithful Charis —

(*CHARIS enters, with TOM, DICK and HORACE. The men are dressed as household slaves.*)

[MUSIC #14 — AT LIBERTY IN THEBES]

(*MUSIC under, as:*)

CHARIS. Let's go, fellas. First drink's on me. Payday!

SOSIA. Charis! What is the meaning of this?

CHARIS. I'm following your instructions. (*To DICK*) Oooh, try that again. Only lower. And slower.

SOSIA. (*To DICK*) Here, unhand her! (*To CHARIS*) What do you mean, *my* instructions?!

CHARIS. Listen to Mr. Innocent! (*MUSIC out.*) Have you forgotten? You told me that from now on, I've got to get my jollies elsewhere.

SOSIA. Wait a second. I'm missing something.

CHARIS. Exactly. But take it from one who knows. It's no great loss. (*MUSIC up; sings*)
THE WORD IS OUT.
THE DIE IS CAST.
I'M SWEARING OFF MY VIRTUOUS PAST
AT LAST!

I'M
AT LIBERTY IN THEBES,
UNINHIBITED AS I CAN BE.
AT LIBERTY IN THEBES—
FOOTLOOSE AND FANCY FREE,
THAT'S ME!
I'VE THROWN OFF ALL MY SHACKLES . . .
CAN'T YOU HEAR THAT CLINKING SOUND?
AT LIBERTY IN THEBES . . .
I'M PROMETHEUS UNBOUND!

MEN.
THE NEWS HAS SPREAD
ALL OVER THE NEIGHBORHOOD.
THE LADY'S GOING BAD . . .
CHARIS.
FOR GOOD!

MEN.
SHE'S
AT LIBERTY IN THEBES . . .
CHARIS.
WITH AN APPETITE TO SATISFY.

Men.
AT LIBERTY IN THEBES . . .
     Charis.
NO LONGER MEEK AND SHY AM I,
I'M OPEN TO SUGGESTION
AND COMPLETELY UNRESTRAINED.
     Men.
AT LIBERTY IN THEBES . . .
     Charis.
I'M AN AMAZON UNCHAINED!

(*SOSIA exits to garden, angrily.*)

     Men.
HERE COMES CHARIS,
READY OR NOT!
     Charis.
SWEET AS A KUMQUAT,
'N HOT TO TROT.
     Men.
CLEAN AS A WHISTLE,
FREE FROM THE POX . . .
     Charis.
AND READY FOR ANYTHING
UNORTHODOX.
     Men.
SHARP AS A THISTLE,
STRONG AS AN OX.
     Charis.
AND TWICE THE TROUBLE OF PANDORA'S BOX!

(*DANCE. CHARIS demonstrates how she plans to make use of
     her new-found freedom. Then:*)

     Men.
AT LIBERTY IN THEBES!
     Charis.
GOVERNED ONLY BY MY OWN CAPRICE.
     Men.
AT LIBERTY IN THEBES!
     Charis.
I AM THE SWEETEST PIECE
IN GREECE!

MEN.
HER LUST HAS BEEN AWAKENED!
CHARIS.
GONNA DANCE FROM NIGHT TIL MORN.
AT LIBERTY IN THEE-EBES . . .
MEN.
AT LIBERTY IN THEE-EBES . . .
CHARIS and MEN.
AT LIBERTY IN THEBES!
CHARIS.
LIKE A PHOENIX . . . I'M REBORN!
CHARIS and MEN.
AT LIBERTY IN THEE-EE-EE-EBES!!!

(*Applause. SOSIA re-enters, carrying a rake. He goes after MEN.*)

SOSIA. Shoo! Away with you! Take a hike!

(*MEN exit. SOSIA retrieves CHARIS's dress, discarded during the dance. He hands it to her, coldly. As she gets dressed:*)

SOSIA. (*continued*) Put your clothes on! This is how you treat me, after a year on the road? Hear me, woman. I will allow no wife of mine to act like this. Running around the neighborhood, like a piece of ancient Greek trash!

(*Lightning and thunder.*)

ALCMENE. (*terrified, from offstage*) Charis!

(*ALCMENE rushes on, from the garden. The gift belt is in her hands.*)

ALCMENE. (*continued*) Charis, take pity on your mistress!
CHARIS. My lady! Whatever is the matter?
ALCMENE. Oh, Charis, I—! (*spotting SOSIA, composing herself*) Sosia. Will you excuse us? Wait in the garden, please?
SOSIA. My lady. (*Glaring at CHARIS, he exits to garden.*)

ALCMENE. (*frantic again*) Tell me quickly! What is this I'm holding?
CHARIS. Why, the beautiful belt your husband presented to you, upon his return last night.
ALCMENE. You are certain? This is the same one?

CHARIS. Of course. Look here. Did he not tell us his initial was engraved on the . . . that's strange. This is not the letter A.
ALCMENE. Not . . . A?
CHARIS. This is the letter J!

(*Lightning and thunder.*)

ALCMENE. J! Heaven protect me! Charis, Amphitryon returned here this morning. Only he acted as if arriving for the first time. He swore he'd never been here last night!
CHARIS. But we all saw him!
ALCMENE. So I told him. Still he persisted, and we parted, bitterly. Then just now, as I sat pondering why he would say such things, I glanced down at the belt. And there was the accursed J!
CHARIS. But of what import—?
ALCMENE. The belt was my proof! Proof Amphitryon had been here, proof I was innocent of any wrongdoing. But now . . .
CHARIS. You fear you were mistaken?
ALCMENE. Never! On my honor as a virtuous woman!
CHARIS. Well, of course. In the dark a woman knows her own husband. It's not like mistaking a knife for a fork.
ALCMENE. And still this curious initial! Oh, Charis. It's not remotely like an A. If I was so wrong in this—dare I say it?—was I wrong about the man I—
CHARIS. My lady!
ALCMENE. I know, I know, it seems absurd. But see how the evidence testifies against me!

[MUSIC #14A—SENNETS IV]

CHARIS. My lady! Your husband approaches!
ALCMENE. Amphitryon? Thank the gods. Leave us!

(*CHARIS exits, with the gift belt.*)

(*Tearfully, ALCMENE runs into the arms of . . . JUPITER!*)

JUPITER. My sweet! Wherefore these tears?
ALCMENE. (*crying, barely intelligible*) I'm so unhappy! Someone came here last night, and I don't know who . . . Tell me, was it you?
JUPITER. What matters who it was? The whole world knows that for Alcmene, there is none other save her Amphitryon.

ALCMENE. Please, torment me no longer. The truth!

JUPITER. Calm yourself. Twas I, no matter who it was. (*explaining*) Whoever appeared to you last night, I know he was Amphitryon to *you*. And whatever favors he received, I know they were meant only for your Amphitryon.

ALCMENE. Then it is true? It was an impostor last night? Oh, how shamefully I have been deceived!

JUPITER. No! He was the one deceived! He imagined you were lying in his arms . . . but in your heart you lay with Amphitryon. He dreamt you were kissing his lips . . . but in your heart, you kissed Amphitryon. He knows all this, believe me, and is so wounded by the fact he may never recover.

ALCMENE. How generous you are! But it is no use. If I can no longer face the world as a virtuous woman, I am unworthy to be your wife. Farewell . . . forever.

JUPITER. Alcmene!

ALCMENE. You can not dissuade me, I go.

JUPITER. Darling!

ALCMENE. Forbear. What was once between us can be no more!

(*She exits.*)

JUPITER. Wait! I shall tell you the truth!

(*ALCMENE re-enters, hand on hip, eyeing JUPITER suspiciously.*)

JUPITER. (*continued*) . . . That is, what I believe to be the truth. Think, my pet. Could any mortal on earth replace Amphitryon in your affections?

ALCMENE. No, never! I swear it!

JUPITER. Well, then. There is only one other alternative. And it exonerates you from blame completely! (*sings*)

[MUSIC #15 — IT MUST HAVE BEEN JOVE]

IT MUST HAVE BEEN JOVE
IN DISGUISE.

ALCMENE. . . . What?

JUPITER.

IT MUST HAVE BEEN JOVE
WHO PULLED THE WOOL
DOWN OVER YOUR EYES.

ALCMENE. Jove? Jupiter Himself?
JUPITER.
ALTHOUGH THE IMPLICATIONS,
I AGREE, ARE IMMENSE,
WE HAVE TO FACE THE FACTS AT HAND
AND USE COMMON SENSE.
HOW ELSE CAN WE EXPLAIN
THE CRAZY TURN OF EVENTS?
IT MUST HAVE BEEN JOVE
IN DISGUISE!

(*He runs off and returns with MERCURY.*)

MERCURY. (*sings*)
IT MUST HAVE BEEN JOVE,
I AGREE.
ALCMENE. . . . Sosia! You really think so?
MERCURY.
IT MUST HAVE BEEN JOVE
WHO LEFT YOU STRANDED
UP IN A TREE.
HE CAME ON A WHIM,
LEFT YOU OUT ON A LIMB.
THOUGH TO SAY IT MAKES ME GULP,
THE CULPRIT MUST HAVE BEEN HIM . . .

(*He points to JUPITER, who quickly pushes MERCURY's hand
    up, so it is pointing at the heavens.*)

JUPITER.
IT MUST HAVE BEEN JOVE,
DON'T YOU SEE?
MERCURY.
IF NOT, THEN WHO ON EARTH COULD IT BE?
JUPITER.
IT'S TRUE THE WHOLE IDEA
IS COMPLETELY ABSURD . . .
MERCURY.
BUT THIS IS NOT THE ONLY TIME
SUCH THINGS HAVE OCCURRED.
JUPITER.
THEY SAY HE CAME TO PRINCESS LEDA—

   MERCURY.
DRESSED LIKE A BIRD.

(*CHARIS appears, to hear:*)

   JUPITER and MERCURY.
IT MUST HAVE BEEN JOVE,
YESSIRREE!

   CHARIS. (*pushing MERCURY aside, sings*)
IT MUST HAVE BEEN JOVE,
LIKE THEY SAID.
IT MUST HAVE BEEN JOVE,
OR YOU'D HAVE KICKED HIM OUT ON HIS HEAD.
YOU'D KNOW HE WAS ODD;
YOU'D SEE THROUGH HIS FACADE.
TO HAVE FOOLED YOU IN THE SACK,
THE BLACKGUARD HAD TO BE GOD!
   JUPITER and MERCURY.
IT MUST HAVE BEEN JOVE
IN YOUR BED!
   CHARIS.
A SHAME IT WASN'T MY BED INSTEAD.
   ALCMENE.
I MUST CONFESS THE NOTION
LEAVES ME TREMBLING WITH AWE.
MY HEART IS ALL A-FLUTTER
AND MY NERVE ENDINGS RAW.
AND YET . . .
   JUPITER, MERCURY and CHARIS. And yet?
   ALCMENE.
WHAT OTHER SANE CONCLUSION CAN WE POSSIBLY
   DRAW?
PERHAPS IT WAS JOVE . . .
   CHARIS.
I'M SURE IT WAS JOVE!
   ALCMENE.
IT MIGHT HAVE BEEN JOVE . . .
   MERCURY.
IT HAD TO BE JOVE!
   ALCMENE.
I GUESS IT WAS JOVE . . .

JUPITER.
I *KNOW* IT WAS JOVE!
    JUPITER and ALL.
IT MUST HAVE BEEN JOVE
IN DISGUISE!

ALCMENE. Oh, Charis! I'm so relieved! No one could fault me for being fooled by a god!
    JUPITER. Of course not. Sosia!

(*SOSIA who has just entered from garden, on his way into the house, answers:*)

SOSIA. Sire?

(*JUPITER, seeing the real SOSIA, employs his cape to shield MERCURY. MERCURY, realizing there are now two "SO-SIAS" rampant, hides behind a pillar.*)

JUPITER. (*to the real SOSIA*) We are to have a great feast, to celebrate the divine blessing which has befallen your mistress. Into town, and summon my generals as dinner guests!
    SOSIA. A sip from the fountain, and I'm off.

(*SOSIA exits to garden, and MERCURY re-enters. MUSIC segues into:*)

[MUSIC #16 — JUPITER SLEPT HERE]

ALCMENE. (*sings*)
ISN'T IT AMAZING?
ISN'T IT A WONDER?
TO THINK WE HAD A VISIT
FROM THE WIELDER OF THE THUNDER!
    JUPITER.
IMAGINE WHAT THE NEIGHBORS WILL SAY
WHEN THEY LEARN WHO STOPPED THIS WAY . . .

(*To the surprise of the principals, DELORES runs on, in her first act finale fur. TOM, DICK and HORACE enter upstage, and dance behind her. The principals, somewhat taken aback, watch stunned as:*)

Delores.
JUPITER SLEPT HERE . . .
RIGHT HERE ON THESE PREMISES.
JUPITER SLEPT HERE . . .
THAT OLD IMMORTAL NEMESIS.
HE CAME DOWN TO EARTH
WITH NO WARNING AT ALL—
THANK HEAVEN SHE WAS HOME
WHEN HE DECIDED TO CALL!
    All but Delores.
THINK OF IT, MY DEAR!
    Delores and All.
JUPITER HIMSELF SLEPT HERE!

(*ALCMENE and the other principals move downstage, trying to
    regain control of the scene.*)

    Alcmene.
BUT WHAT WAS THE REASON FOR HIS VISIT?
    Charis.
JOVE MUST HAVE FALLEN IN LOVE!
    Jupiter.
YES, HE SAW YOU FROM ABOVE,
AND THOUGHT YOU WERE EXQUISITE . . .

(*SOSIA enters from garden, and joins the song.*)

    Mercury and Sosia.
BUT KNOWING WHAT A RAKE HE IS,
IT'S NOT SURPRISING, IS IT?

(*MERCURY hides again, before anyone notices there are two
    SOSIAS.*)

(*THE CHORUS, led by DELORES moves forward, again in-
    truding on the principals.*)

    All but Alcmene.
JUPITER SLEPT HERE . . .
RIGHT IN THIS LOCALITY.
JUPITER SLEPT HERE . . .
ALTHOUGH IT STRAINS REALITY.

Charis.
THE PARCEL OF LAND
IS NO MORE THAN THIRD-RATE . . .
Sosia.
BUT THANKS TO JOVE
IT'S NOW A PIECE OF UNREAL ESTATE!
Alcmene. Wait!

(*All activity ceases. ALCMENE comes forward; this is her big moment. She throws a warning look at DELORES, then turns to JUPITER.*)

Alcmene. (*continued*) You mean Jupiter came down and spent the night . . . out of *sheer whim*?
Jupiter. Well, yes. At first. But then he fell madly, wildly in love with you. And tell the truth. Don't you love him too?
Alcmene. After he deceived me? I hate Jupiter! Why couldn't he stay up in heaven where he belongs!

(*Weeping, she runs into the palace. JUPITER clutches his heart, as if mortally wounded. A pause, then:*)

Delores. (*getting the action started again*) 5-6-7-8!
All but Jupiter.
GOD KNOWS WHAT WE'LL CLEAR
IF WE WAIT TO SELL TIL NEXT YEAR!
EVERYBODY CHEER!
JUPITER . . . JUPITER . . . JUPITER
SLEPT HERE!

(*During the final bars, the following takes place:*)

(*TOM, DICK and HORACE assume a final pose.*)

(*SOSIA moves over to join DELORES, and puts his arms around her, flirting. DELORES giggles, calling to Murray out in the audience, as if to say "Isn't he cute?"*)

(*MERCURY re-enters, to console his father.*)

(*CHARIS spots the two SOSIAS.*)

(*JUPITER collapses into MERCURY's arms, overcome with grief.*)

BLACKOUT

END ACT I

ACT TWO

[MUSIC #17 — BACK TO THE PLAY]

As the intermission is drawing to a close, the vamp to "WEL-
COME TO GREECE" begins. DELORES leads on the rest
of THE CHORUS.

DELORES. (*shouted*) Let's go!
THE CHORUS. (*sings*)
BACK TO YOUR SEAT!
BACK TO YOUR SEAT!
PLEASE, EVERYBODY TAKE A SEAT.
WE ARE THE CHORUS . . .
TOM, DICK AND HORACE.
DELORES.
MY NAME'S DELORES . . .
THE CHORUS.
BACK TO YOUR SEAT!

(*MUSIC continues vamping, as DELORES steps forward and*
addresses the audience as it continues to file in. TOM, DICK
and HORACE stand behind her, bouncing in place.)

DELORES. Come on in, everyone. The second act is starting,
and I wouldn't want you to miss anything. You all remember
where you were sitting? Good. Have you all met Murray? No?
Gee, that's funny. He usually stands right back there. Make sure
you see him after the show. He's handing out maps, so you can
all come down and visit our salon on Avenue J. This week only
we're having a special 10% discount on everything in the store.
It's our special __________* Sale. And if you come on Sunday,
we serve bagels and cappucino. Okay, everybody ready?
TOM, DICK and HORACE. Ready!

THE CHORUS. (*resuming the number*)
AND NOW THE PLAY . . .
BACK TO THE PLAY!

---

*Substitute nearest holiday (i.e. Labor Day, Arbor Day, Valentine's Day, Rosh
Hashana, Back to School, etc.)

58

Tom.
MADAM, HURRY PLEASE, WE HAVEN'T GOT ALL DAY.
The Chorus.
WE ARE THE CHORUS.
PLEASE DO THIS FOR US?
Delores.
I'M STILL DELORES . . .
The Chorus.
BACK TO THE PLAY!

(*MUSIC continues under as:*)

Tom. (*stepping forward*) Well, the cat is out of the bag. Jupiter has come to earth and spent the night with Princess Alcmene.
Delores. (*to Tom*) God bless you.
Dick. In celebration, a great feast has been planned . . .

(*CHARIS enters, proudly displaying two scrawny rubber chickens, and exits. SOSIA enters.*)

Horace. . . . And Sosia has been sent to fetch the dinner guests.
Sosia. (*to audience, deadpan*) I wanna tell you. We ancient Greeks — the fun just never stops.

(*He kisses DELORES on the cheek and exits.*)

The Chorus.
ON WITH THE SHOW!
ON WITH THE SHOW . . .
NOW THAT YOU KNOW THE STATUS QUO.
WE ARE THE CHORUS . . .
Delores. (*pointing them out*)
TOM, DICK AND HORACE!
Tom, Dick and Horace.
YOU KNOW DELORES . . .
The Chorus.
AWAY WE GO!!!

(*Applause. THE CHORUS exits. A distraught JUPITER enters, followed by MERCURY.*)

Mercury. Father, you have got to snap out of this!

JUPITER. It's over, Mercury. My whole life is over. The only woman I've ever loved, and she despises me.

MERCURY. She doesn't despise you. She is hurt and she is angry. But she'll forgive you.

JUPITER. If only I could believe that!

MERCURY. She will. There is not a doubt in my mind!

(*ALCMENE enters and addresses the heavens.*)

ALCMENE. I'll never forgive you, Jupiter. Never, ever, ever!

MERCURY. Well, it might take a little time . . .

ALCMENE. Never! Not in a million, zillion years!

(*ALCMENE exits.*)

JUPITER. I can't endure it, Mercury. My heart is breaking. I'm going to end it all! (*Melodramatically, he jumps up on a bench and draws his sword.*)

MERCURY. You can't end it all. We're immortal.

JUPITER. Oh, yes. I forgot. How cruel the fates are! And how foolish, imagining she could love an unworthy creature such as I.

MERCURY. I will not have you talking like that about yourself. Have you forgotten who you are?

JUPITER. Who am I? Unloved, unwanted. You're nobody til somebody loves you.

MERCURY. Nonsense. You are Eternal Ruler of the Universe.

JUPITER. Big deal. Is that any reason to love me?

MERCURY. Don't be ridiculous. Look at this beautiful world you've created. Those spacious skies. That fruited plain. The sun in the morning and the moon at night.

JUPITER. (*moving away, moodily*) A lot of good it does me.

[MUSIC #18 — SOMETHING OF YOURSELF
(DON'T BRING HER FLOWERS)]

MERCURY. Face facts, Father. The woman knows nothing of your true nature. If she is to love you, you must give her something more to go on.

JUPITER. Give her something . . . Of course! And I know just the thing! Flowers. Women love flowers!

MERCURY. (*sings*)
DON'T BRING HER FLOWERS
TO BRIGHTEN UP THE ROOM.
DON'T BE ONE WHO SHOWERS
HER WITH CANDY AND PERFUME.
IF YOU YEARN FOR HER AFFECTIONS,
SIMPLY FOLLOW THESE DIRECTIONS:
GIVE HER SOMETHING OF YOURSELF.

DON'T SING HER PRAISES,
OR OVERLOOK HER FLAWS.
EASY, EMPTY PHRASES
WILL NOT WIN HER TO YOUR CAUSE.
TO ASSURE HER ADMIRATION
WITHOUT PAUSE OR RESERVATION—
OFFER SOMETHING OF YOURSELF.

OPEN YOUR HEART TO HER . . .
UNLOCK THE DOOR.
SHOW THE SIDE THAT PEOPLE RARELY SEE.
TRY TO IMPART TO HER
NOT JUST WHO YOU ARE,
BUT ALL YOU LONG TO BE.

LET HER DISCOVER
THE YOU THAT NO ONE KNOWS.
WITH EACH SECRET YOU UNCOVER,
THE MORE HER ARDOR GROWS.
LOVE WILL BLOOM IN QUICK SUCCESSION
ONCE YOU SHARE THAT PRIZED POSSESSION:
A LITTLE SOMETHING OF YOURSELF.

(*MUSIC continues under:*)

JUPITER. But how do I begin? What do I say?

MERCURY. Oh, you'll think of something. For starters, why not tell her your real reasons for coming down to earth?

JUPITER. But it's only for a lark. Fun and frolic, nothing more . . .

MERCURY. Is it, Father? Don't you come down here, time after time, hoping to find something else?

JUPITER. I can't imagine what you're talking about.

Mercury. Very well. Have it your own way. But think about it, won't you? You know, anyone who got to know the real Jupiter couldn't help but adore him.

DON'T BRING HER FLOWERS
IF YOU WANT MY ADVICE.
LOVE REQUIRES MORE THAN FLOWERS . . .
IT TAKES SOME SACRIFICE.
AND ONE THING THAT MAY SURPRISE YOU?
YOU MAY FIND IT GRATIFIES YOU
TO GIVE UP SOMETHING OF YOURSELF.

(*Applause. TOM, DICK and HORACE rush on.*)

[MUSIC #19 — ENTER THE HUSBAND II]

Tom, Dick and Horace. (*sing*)
ENTER THE HUSBAND . . .
   Jupiter. Now?!
   Tom, Dick and Horace.
ENTER THE HUSBAND . . .
   Jupiter. (*to MERCURY, exiting*) Tell them to keep singing!
   Tom, Dick and Horace.
ENTER! ENTER!
ENTER THE HUSBAND . . .
(*MERCURY mimes looking off at the approaching AMPHI-TRYON.*)
ENTER THE HUSBAND!
(*MERCURY exits.*)
ENTER THE HUSBAND!

ENTER! ENTER!
ENTER THE HUSBAND!

(*A crash is heard offstage, followed by the sotto voce whisper of the actor playing JUPITER/AMPHITRYON: "Where's my helmet?"*)

(*DELORES runs on, giggling apologetically.*)

   Delores. He'll be out in a minute!

(*DELORES exits. TOM, DICK and HORACE smile, a bit sheep-*
ishly. They shrug, and try again.)

Tom, Dick and Horace.
ENTER! ENTER!
ENTER THE HUSBAND!

(*AMPHITRYON rushes on, his helmet covering his face. The*
helmet is askew. But it is AMPHITRYON.)

Amphitryon. Curse the heavens!

(*TOM, DICK and HORACE, visibly relieved, exit. AMPHIT-*
RYON removes his helmet.)

Amphitryon. (*continued*) I have yet to tell my men of the
strange events that have transpired. Of a belt that disappears
from a well-sealed pouch, or of a wife who mistakes another man
for her husband. Instead, I have returned here, in the vain hope
further inquiry may shed new light. Despite what I heard earlier,
every fiber of my being rebels. Alcmene, unfaithful? Never! Nay,
tis either a misunderstanding, or some evil sorcerer has bewitched
her. And if that be the case, let the demon beware! Behold, the
blade of Amphitryon! (*He draws his sword, impressively. After*
a moment, he wavers.)
Courage, Amphitryon. Even if she has been unfaithful, you
must know the truth.

[MUSIC #19A — INTO THE PALACE]

(*Replacing his sword, he marches off into the palace. Three*
knocks. After a moment, he returns.)

Amphitryon. (*continued*) Strange. Why should the house be
locked at this time of day? (*sings*)

[MUSIC #20 — OPEN UP]

OPEN UP
IN THE NAME OF AMPHITRYON.
UNLOCK THE DOOR WITHOUT DELAY.
OPEN UP

IN THE NAME OF AMPHITRYON . . .
AMPHITRYON IS HERE TO SAVE THE DAY!

(*MERCURY enters.*)

MERCURY.
PIPE DOWN
IN THE NAME OF HEAVEN . . .
DO US ALL A FAVOR?
GO AWAY!

(*MERCURY exits.*)

AMPHITRYON. Has every man in Thebes lost his wits? Sosia!
MERCURY. (*re-entering*) You called?
AMPHITRYON. Don't you see me?
MERCURY. Clear as day. What's your problem, Amph?
AMPHITRYON. Rascal! I'll teach you how to address me!

(*AMPHITRYON draws his sword and goes after MERCURY,
who exits* S.L.)

(*At the same time, SOSIA enters* S.R., *followed by DICK, HOR-
ACE and DELORES, all dressed as Theban GENERALS.
DELORES wears a golden breastplate encrusted with glitter
and rhinestones, and edged in maribou. Her helmet is huge
and is adorned with garishly colored feathers.*)

SOSIA. Here I am, sire. With all the dinner guests I could find.

(*AMPHITRYON whirls around to face the real SOSIA. He looks
off at where MERCURY has exited, then back to SOSIA.*)

AMPHITRYON. You! Again?!
SOSIA. Right on schedule. What's for dinner? I'm starved!
AMPHITRYON. Traitor! Prepare to die!
SOSIA. Oh, no. Charis fixed that awful cabbage stew again.
AMPHITRYON. Swine! You know who I am now?
SOSIA. What slave doesn't know his own master?
AMPHITRYON. So you knew all along? Viper . . . you are
doomed!

(*AMPHITRYON throws a bewildered SOSIA to the ground, and raises his sword.*)

(*The GENERALS rush to restrain AMPHITRYON.*)

[MUSIC #21 — O, STAY YOUR HAND]

GENERALS. (*sing*)
O, STAY YOUR HAND,
AMPHITRYON!
AMPHITRYON,
EXERCISE RESTRAINT!

(*DELORES does a little showgirl "bump" at the end of each section.*)

AMPHITRYON. Don't meddle. This is between him and me.
SOSIA. Please, be my guests! Meddle, meddle!
GENERALS.
O, STAY YOUR HAND,
AMPHITRYON . . .
UNTIL WE ARE ACQUAINTED
WITH YOUR COMPLAINT!

SOSIA. Yes, how have I offended you?
AMPHITRYON. How?
DELORES. Yes, *how*?
AMPHITRYON. He locked me from my own house, and displayed an insolent manner worthy of execution. And you shall pay, rascal!

GENERALS.
O, NOBLE LORD
AMPHITRYON,
WE CAN SPEAK IN SOSIA'S DEFENSE.
HE'S BEEN WITH US IN CAMP
THIS HOUR HENCE.

AMPHITRYON. In camp?
SOSIA. As you ordered me!
AMPHITRYON. I? When?

SOSIA. After making peace with my lady! A great feast was planned, and I was sent to invite all the guests.

AMPHITRYON. By Jove! Every step takes me deeper into the labyrinthe. Who will help me in my hour of need?

(*MUSIC under, as the GENERALS bow to their commanding officer. DELORES is last, and does a supportive bump and grind.*)

AMPHITRYON. (*continued*) Friends, I welcome your help. Together, we shall solve this infernal puzzle.

[MUSIC #22 — GENERALS PANDEMONIUM]

(*GENERALS stand, as AMPHITRYON starts into palace. He stops, looking off.*)

AMPHITRYON. (*continued*) By the gods! You!

(*He exits and JUPITER, wearing his wreath, comes hurtling on-stage, as if ejected from the palace by AMPHITRYON.*)

JUPITER. (*sings*)
WHO IS THIS WHO COMES A-KNOCKING?
SUCH BEHAVIOR! TRULY SHOCKING!
STATE YOUR BUSINESS, FELON, AND BEGONE!

(*JUPITER rushes back into the palace.*)

SOSIA and GENERALS. (*sing*)
AMPHITRYON! AMPHITRYON! AMPHITRYON!

(*AMPHITRYON, holding his helmet, comes hurtling out of the palace, as if he has been tossed out by JUPITER.*)

AMPHITRYON.
HERE'S THE ROOT OF ALL OUR TROUBLE —
ON MY SOUL, A PERFECT DOUBLE!
WHAT A STRANGE AND FRIGHTENING PHENOMENON!

(*AMPHITRYON rushes back into the palace.*)

Sosia and Generals.
AMPHITRYON! AMPHITRYON! AMPHITRYON!

(*During the following, we see JUPITER at the entrance to the palace, being choked by an offstage, unseen "AMPHITRYON." JUPITER exits and then AMPHITRYON appears, using his helmet to fight an offstage, unseen "JUPITER."*)

Sosia and Generals.
NOW WHAT DO WE DO?
THE WORLD HAS GONE ASKEW!
INSTEAD OF ONE AMPHITRYON,
TWO COME INTO VIEW.
ONE IS FALSE, THE OTHER TRUE . . .
JOVE ALONE KNOWS WHICH IS WHO.
BUT WE MUST SEE IT THROUGH . . .

(*JUPITER stumbles out of palace.*)

Sosia and Generals.
SO TELL US, WHO ARE YOU?
Jupiter.
AMPHITRYON!

(*JUPITER returns to the palace.*)

Sosia and Generals.
AMPHITRYON! AMPHITRYON!
AMPHITRYON! AMPHITRYON!

(*AMPHITRYON stumbles back on.*)

Sosia and Generals.
AND YOU?
Amphitryon.
AMPHITRYON!
Sosia and Generals.
AMPHIT—AMPHIT—AMPHITRYON!

(*JUPITER emerges from the palace wrestling with "AMPHITRYON."*)

(*NOTE: The actor playing TOM plays the "AMPHITRYON" double. He wears a costume identical to JUPITER, but with AMPHITRYON's helmet pushed down over his face.*)

(*SOSIA and GENERALS join hands, a la "Swan Lake" and dance as:*)

Generals.
NOW WE'RE IN A STEW . . .
Sosia.
NOW WE'RE IN A STEW!
Generals.
WHO KNOWS WHAT WILL ENSUE?
Sosia.
WHO KNOWS WHAT WILL ENSUE?
Sosia and Generals.
THEY BOTH CLAIM THEY'RE AMPHITRYON . . .
WHAT CAN WE CONSTRUE?

Generals.
ONE IS FALSE . . .
Sosia.
ONE IS FALSE!
Generals.
THE OTHER TRUE.
Sosia.
THE OTHER TRUE!
Sosia and Generals.
JOVE ALONE KNOWS WHICH IS WHO.
OH, IF WE ONLY KNEW . . .
BUT WE DON'T HAVE A CLUE!

(*GENERALS manage to separate the battling JUPITER and "AMPHITRYON." "AMPHITRYON" is restrained by DELORES and DICK.*)

Sosia.
O, NOBLE LORDS OF THEBES,
SET YOUR MINDS TO REST.
SURELY YOU AGREE
A LOYAL SLAVE LIKE ME
KNOWS HIS MASTER BEST?

AND AS TO WHICH IS HE,
I HAVE NO DOUBT.
(*pointing to JUPITER*)
HERE IS THE GENUINE ARTICLE!
(*pointing to AMPHITRYON*)
THROW THE IMPOSTOR OUT!

[MUSIC #22A — PANDEMONIUM PLAYOFF]

(*MUSIC continues under as "AMPHITRYON" breaks loose of his restraints and rushes after SOSIA, then turns and goes after JUPITER. JUPITER rushes into palace, followed by "AMPHITRYON," the GENERALS and then SOSIA. Pause. SOSIA reemerges, and then AMPHITRYON is tossed out of the palace. His helmet is thrown out after him.*)

AMPHITRYON. (*catching the helmet*) Go then, traitors. Honor the impostor! I have other friends in Thebes. And with their help, I shall take my revenge. For I shall *have* my revenge!

(*Glaring at SOSIA, he exits.*)

SOSIA. Peace at last. And now for some dinner. I still haven't eaten anything.

(*SOSIA exits into palace. MERCURY enters, holding SOSIA by the ear.*)

SOSIA. Can't we talk this over? We have so much in common. You and I should be friends.
MERCURY. Surely you jest? I, consort with the likes of you?
SOSIA. Why not? You *are* the likes of me.

(*CHARIS enters, and spots the two "SOSIAS."*)

CHARIS. All right. Nobody move.

[MUSIC #23 — TWO SOSIAS]

(*sings*)
TWO SOSIAS! TWO SOSIAS!
I KNEW I SAW TWO SOSIAS!

ONE OF THEM IS MINE—
THE OTHER MUST BE DIVINE.
TWO SOSIAS! TWO SOSIAS!
IT'S TRUE I SAW TWO SOSIAS . . .
SURELY IT'S A SIGN?
A GOD HAS COME TO CALL ON ME
AND WORSHIP AT MY SHRINE!
Okay, fellas. Quit stalling. Who's the lucky impostor who gets to share my bed?

SOSIA and MERCURY. He is!

(*Both men dash for the palace. SOSIA gets out first, but [unseen by CHARIS] MERCURY zaps SOSIA and magically pulls him back on stage. Then, MERCURY exits.*)

(*CHARIS turns to the dazed SOSIA.*)

CHARIS.
IT'S YOU! THE GOD!
I SEE THROUGH YOUR DISGUISE!
HOW FRIGHT'NING,
THE LIGHTNING
THAT'S COMING FROM YOUR EYES.
IT'S YOU! THE GOD!
I WON MYSELF A PRIZE!
OH, TAKE ME SIRE.
MY HEART'S AFIRE.
YOUR EVERY WISH IS MY DESIRE . . .
SOSIA. Oh, pull yourself together, woman! You can't really believe I'm—(*CHARIS swoons into his arms.*) Charis! Wake up! Are you all right?
CHARIS. Forgive me, your Godship. I became faint in your divine presence.
SOSIA. It does that to a lot of people.
CHARIS. Then it's true? I am to receive a night of celestial bliss?

(*SOSIA mulls it over a moment, then decides to seize the opportunity.*)

SOSIA. That's right, baby. This is the big one. Hold on to your tunic.

[MUSIC #24 — HEAVEN ON EARTH (REPRISE)]

(*sings*)
BABY . . . BABY . . .
PUT YOUR TRUST IN ME.
I CAN GUARANTEE
TONIGHT WILL BE . . .
HEAVEN ON EARTH!
  SOSIA and CHARIS.
HEAVEN ON EARTH!
  SOSIA.
WE WILL TAKE TO THE SKY . . .
  CHARIS.
WE WILL FLY, YOU AND I . . .
  CHARIS and SOSIA.
WE WILL LEAVE THIS WORLD BEHIND!
  SOSIA.
DEEP IN THE NIGHT WE'LL FIND . . .
  SOSIA and CHARIS.
BODIES AND SOULS ENTWINED!
FIRE AND ICE COMBINED . . .

(*MUSIC segues into a slow, seductive tango. SOSIA starts off
    to garden, looks back at CHARIS suggestively, and exits.
    Ecstatic, CHARIS runs off to join him.*)

(*Applause.*)

[MUSIC #24A — SCENE CHANGE]

(*A nervous JUPITER enters from the palace, talking with MER-
    CURY. The gods see someone coming, and MERCURY
    dashes off.*)

(*ALCMENE enters from the palace. MUSIC out.*)

ALCMENE. Amphitryon? Sosia said you wanted to see me?
JUPITER. Yes. Yes, my sweet. A few moments of your time. . .?
ALCMENE. Of course, dearest. But what of our guests?
JUPITER. The servants will tend to them. I . . . I would have a
word with you. About Jupiter.

ALCMENE. Jupiter? That unfeeling monster you call a god? That lying, deceitful—

JUPITER. Please, don't say that! He's not the way you think!

ALCMENE. Isn't he?

JUPITER. No! He never meant to deceive you on purpose.

ALCMENE. Then why did he assume a disguise?

JUPITER. He always does that when he comes to earth. He can't reveal his . . . true self.

ALCMENE. Why not?

JUPITER. (*looking away, with difficulty*) Because. He's . . . too shy.

ALCMENE. Shy. The Supreme Ruler of the Universe . . . is shy?

JUPITER. Ironic, isn't it? The man can toss around thunderbolts but he just can't handle rejection.

[MUSIC #24B — OLYMPUS UNDERSCORE]

(*MUSIC under. ALCMENE's hurt feelings start to dissipate.*)

ALCMENE. Imagine that. It makes him seem almost human . . .

JUPITER. He is! Even more than he suspected.

ALCMENE. Amphitryon . . . how do you know so much about Jupiter?

JUPITER. How do I know? (*MUSIC out.*) . . . Princess Leda. Close friend of the family. Oh darling, can't you forgive Jupiter? Accept his visit as the blessing he intended it to be?

ALCMENE. I suppose. Only—do not be angry with me?—but could I turn time back, I would still wish Jupiter had never come between us.

JUPITER. Still?!

ALCMENE. With all my heart!

(*Unseen by ALCMENE, JUPITER throws a small tantrum, hopping about and drumming his head with his fists. He recovers just as ALCMENE turns to him, and forces a smile. But his smile soon evaporates, and he sits, forlornly. MUSIC under:*)

JUPITER. (*with a heavy heart*) Alcmene. Have you any notion what it's like . . . being Eternal Ruler of the Universe?

ALCMENE. No. I've never given it much thought . . .

JUPITER. No, few people do. They assume it's one long endless round of parties up in heaven.

ALCMENE. Isn't it? (*MUSIC out.*)
JUPITER. Well, they have a few parties. But you've no idea of the pressures upon Jupiter. Keeping the cosmos in order.

[MUSIC #25 — OLYMPUS IS A LONELY TOWN]

JUPITER. (*continued*) Maintaining the harmony of the heavens. Believe me. Being god isn't all it's cracked up to be. (*sings*)

HE SITS, ALL ALONE,
ON A HIGH-PLACED THRONE
BASKING IN ACCLAIM AND RENOWN.
YOU'D THINK HE WAS ON TOP OF THE WORLD . . .
BUT OLYMPUS IS A LONELY TOWN.

HE STANDS AT THE HELM
OF A FAR-FLUNG REALM —
SO WHY SHOULD HE BE WEARING A FROWN?
HE'D SEEM WITHOUT A CARE IN THE WORLD . . .
BUT OLYMPUS IS ONE TOWN
THAT GETS YOU DOWN.

THE GLAMOUR? THE CLAMOR? THE ADULATION?
ALL SO MANY TROPHIES ON THE SHELF.
THE POETS SING OF GLORY —
BUT WHAT'S THE INSIDE STORY?
OH, HOW HE LONGS TO BE LOVED FOR HIMSELF!

HIS EMPIRE IS VAST,
RICHES UNSURPASSED,
BUT ON HIS HEAD HE WEARS A HOLLOW CROWN.
THIS MAY COME TO YOU AS NEWS,
BUT HE OFTEN SINGS THE BLUES . . .
OLYMPUS IS ONE SAD AND LONELY TOWN!

(*Applause. ALCMENE is visibly moved.*)

[MUSIC #26 — SOMETHING OF YOURSELF (REPRISE)]

ALCMENE. Oh. Poor Jupiter! I never realized . . .
JUPITER. And that's only the half of it! Believe me, it's not all nectar and ambrosia . . .

(*ALCMENE and JUPITER sit, as the lights begin to dim. MER-
     CURY enters, with TOM, DICK and HORACE. They stand
     in front of ALCMENE and JUPITER, and sing:*)

     MERCURY.
OPEN YOUR HEART TO HER . . .
UNLOCK THE DOOR.
SHOW THE SIDE THAT PEOPLE RARELY SEE.
     MEN.
TRY TO IMPART TO HER
NOT JUST WHO YOU ARE . . .
     MERCURY and MEN.
TELL HER ALL YOU LONG TO BE.

LET HER DISCOVER
THE YOU THAT NO ONE KNOWS.
WITH EACH SECRET YOU UNCOVER,
THE MORE HER ARDOR GROWS.
     MERCURY.
LOVE WILL BLOOM IN QUICK SUCCESSION
ONCE YOU SHARE THAT PRIZED POSSESSION:
     MERCURY and MEN.
A LITTLE SOMETHING OF YOURSELF . . .

(*MERCURY and MEN exit. Lights come up on JUPITER who
     is now lying down, as if on an analyst's couch, with his head
     in ALCMENE's lap.*)

     JUPITER. . . . and of course, Mother Earth never really under-
stood him.
     ALCMENE. And how did he *feel* about that?
     JUPITER. How do you think he felt? He created a whole uni-
verse, and it still wasn't enough.
     ALCMENE. Amphitryon, I'm afraid our time is up. We must
tend to our guests. But I want you to know . . . I forgive Jupiter.
     JUPITER. You do?
     ALCMENE. And I love you . . . for being so sensitive to his
feelings.
     JUPITER. You love me? Oh, my precious! (*He starts to kiss
her, then a worrisome thought strikes him.*)
     Alcmene? What would happen if another Amphitryon — be-
sides me, of course — were suddenly to appear?

ALCMENE. *Another* Amphitryon?! That would have to be the god . . . that poor lonely creature who showed up last night.

JUPITER. Could you love him . . . as much as you love me?

ALCMENE. Don't be silly. There is only one man I want for my husband. And you, my dearest, are that man. (*Overjoyed, JUPITER kisses her.*)

Come, we're being rude to our guests. (*starts out, then:*)

You know something, Amphitryon? If Jupiter starts to feel lonely again, I really do hope he comes back to visit. I could introduce him to some lovely girls.

(*ALCMENE exits.*)

JUPITER. (*looking around*) Mercury! Mercury, where are you?

MERCURY. (*entering*) Here I am, Father. I'm right here.

JUPITER. Were you listening? She loves me. She loves *me*! She wants me for her husband.

MERCURY. I'm delirious for you both. Can we return to heaven now?

JUPITER. What a woman! What an entrancing creature! What a shame she has so little time left on earth!

MERCURY. So little time . . . ? What are you planning?

JUPITER. Remember that sector to the left of Sagittarius? That's where I'm placing my new "Alcmene Constellation!"

MERCURY. You're joking . . . I hope.

JUPITER. Not at all. I love her! I'm not going to watch her in the arms of another man every night!

MERCURY. Oh, I was afraid of this. You've discovered another human emotion. Jealousy!

JUPITER. Have I? I *am* clever.

MERCURY. Father, you can't do this. It's not fair.

JUPITER. I don't have to be fair. It's my universe. You don't like it, play somewhere else!

MERCURY. But you're being so selfish. What will people think?

JUPITER. What do I care . . . so long as I can see the princess in heaven for all eternity?

MERCURY. And what of her husband?

JUPITER. Him I'll see in Hades.

MERCURY. Father, we are gods. We're supposed to set an example!

JUPITER. Would you challenge me? (*JUPITER raises his arm. Lightning and thunder.*) Good, then it is settled. Once the husband returns, I shall reveal my true identity. And then . . . I'm going to make that girl a star!

[MUSIC #27 — A STAR IS BORN]

(*Quick blackout, as JUPITER and MERCURY exit. Stars are seen in the sky. A spotlight picks up DELORES, who wears a full-length black mink coat. She smiles at us, innocently.*)

DELORES. . . . Did someone mention "star?" (*sings*)
TELL THE GODS
UP IN HEAVEN . . .
LET THEM KNOW
NEAR AND FAR.
GUESS WHO IS MAKING HER DEBUT?

(*She flashes her coat, revealing a quick glance at the gown she is wearing underneath.*)

A BRAND NEW STAR!

SHE BELONGS
UP IN HEAVEN
WHERE THOSE
OTHER STARS ARE.
SHE'LL SOON BE COMING INTO VIEW . . .

(*DELORES removes her fur coat. She is wearing a full-length silver sequinned gown with star appliques, and silver gloves and shoes.*)

A BRAND NEW,
GRAND NEW STAR!

GET READY, URSA MAJOR!
YOU'RE IN FOR SURPRISE.
I WOULD BE WILLING TO WAGER
THIS GAL WILL DAZZLE YOUR EYES!

STRIKE THE BAND
UP IN HEAVEN.
POUND THE DRUM!

SOUND THE HORN!
AND KEEP YOUR EYES ON THE HORIZON . . .
TONIGHT, A STAR IS BORN!

(*Suddenly, TOM, DICK, HORACE enter, along with JUPI-
TER, MERCURY and SOSIA. The six men sport silver sequinned hats, canes, and silver lamé capes.*)

(*All have forced smiles, obviously having been pressed into ser-
vice for this number as a courtesy to producer "MURRAY
THE FURRIER."*)

MEN.
THOSE WHO SHINE
UP IN HEAVEN
MUST BE WELL
ABOVE PAR . . .

(*DELORES is apparently shocked by their appearance. She is so
moved at her husband's generosity, tears well up in her eyes.*)

DELORES. Oh, Murray! Did you do this for me?!
MEN.
SHE SOON WILL JOIN THE CHOSEN FEW . . .
A BRAND NEW
GRAND NEW STAR!

(*MEN begin to dance around DELORES in a circle, as ALC-
MENE and CHARIS enter, also in top hats and capes. At
the same time, a silver foil drop flies in upstage.*)

SHE'S LEAVING EARTH BEHIND HER
TO DWELL WITH THOSE ON HIGH.
TWINKLING ABOVE'S WHERE YOU'LL FIND HER . . .
DELORES.
GUESS WHO WILL LIGHT UP THE SKY?

(*ALL join in what has now become a traditional "hats-off to the
leading lady" number. And to cap it off, chaser lights which
ring the columns and the proscenium arch begin to twinkle
madly as:*)

COMPANY.
RAISE THE ROOF
UP IN HEAVEN.
LIVE IT UP.
GIVE A CHEER.
SOMETHING EARTHSHAKING'S
IN THE MAKING.
TONIGHT'S THE BIG PREMIERE.
SHE'LL APPEAR ON THE SCENE
RIGHT IN BETWEEN
LEO AND CAPRICORN.
ONLY MOMENTS FROM NOW,
SHE'LL BE TAKING HER BOW.
TONIGHT, A STAR IS . . .

(*A tympani roll, as:*)

DELORES. (*overcome*) Murray . . . I love you!!!

COMPANY.
. . . BORN!!!

(*Applause. Direct segue into:*)

[MUSIC #27A — A STAR IS BORN (PLAYOFF)]

COMPANY.
SHE'LL APPEAR ON THE SCENE
RIGHT IN BETWEEN
LEO AND CAPRICORN.
ONLY MOMENTS FROM NOW
SHE'LL BE TAKING HER BOW.
TONIGHT . . . A STAR IS BORN!

(*DELORES is the last to exit, blowing kisses and thanking the
     audience. She retrieves her fur, mistakenly walks into the
     proscenium arch, giggles and exits. By now, the chaser lights
     have faded, the silver drop has flown out, and we are back
     into the play.*)

(*SOSIA enters from the garden, barely able to walk, and ob-*

viously exhausted. CHARIS, glowing, enters and exhales cigarette smoke.)

CHARIS. Oh. Oh, your Celestialship. I still can't believe my good fortune. To think: I have known a god.

SOSIA. Amazing, isn't it? Well, it's really been delightful bringing some sunshine into your life . . . but now I must be going.

CHARIS. Going? But your Godliness . . . we were just getting started.

SOSIA. Sorry. I got a hot date with a wood nymph.

CHARIS. You mean . . . there's someone else?

SOSIA. Charis . . . when you're as good as I am, it's only fair to spread it around.

CHARIS. Yes, I suppose so. But your Awesomeness . . . couldn't we try it again? Just one more time?

SOSIA. Are you serious? Twice in one day? I might do permanent damage. To both of us.

CHARIS. But your Magnificence . . . surely, one more round of —

SOSIA. Charis, have a heart, will you? A mortal man can do so much. I'm only human! (*Too late he realizes his slip. CHARIS peers at him.*)

CHARIS. . . . Sosia? Sosia!? Why, you little fraud!

SOSIA. I tried to tell you. You wouldn't listen.

CHARIS. To think: I believed *you* were a god. How ridiculous!

SOSIA. Why? You sure seemed to buy it back there in the garden! You think a real god would've been so much different? You know something? You wouldn't know a real god if you saw one face to face!

CHARIS. I know this much. After all I've suffered . . . I deserve a bigger reward than that!

(CHARIS exits. SOSIA goes in after her. MERCURY meets him at the door, and tosses him out.)

MERCURY. . . . And stay out!

(MERCURY exits. Painfully, SOSIA dusts himself off.)

[MUSIC #28 — HAILS]

(AMPHITRYON, wearing his helmet, enters. DICK and HOR-

ACE, dressed as CITIZENS OF THEBES follow him on, singing:)

DICK and HORACE.
HAIL TO GENERAL AMPHITRYON!
WHO IN THE WORLD IS HIS PEER?

(DELORES runs on, obviously a bit late for her cue. She is dressed as HIGH PRIESTESS OF THEBES, and wears a scanty leopard skin and a Cleopatra headdress, replete with golden snakes. She takes her place next to DICK and HOR-ACE, nervously. This is her "big scene." Throughout, she mouths the words of the other characters, awaiting her cues.)

AMPHITRYON. Friends! You are here to bear witness against a foul fiend — an impostor who would drive me from Thebes and my wife's affections. Therefore, look upon me and say: who am I?

HIGH PRIESTESS. Worthy lord! (*She steps forward. She may well be the worst actress ever to trod the boards.*) Worthy lord! Do you imagine I, High Priestess of Thebes, would disavow the savior of our fair city? Citizens . . . hail to General Amphitryon!

DICK and HORACE. Hail to General Amphitryon!

AMPHITRYON. Thank you.

HIGH PRIESTESS. You're welcome.

AMPHITRYON. Now. When this demon appears, you may yet fall prey to his deception. To remind you who I am . . . I shall bend my helmet plume!

HIGH PRIESTESS. My liege . . . this is uncalled for! I have known you since you were a boy. Let this impostor come before me. By all that is holy, I shall denounce him, and see him doomed to destruction! Or worse!

AMPHITRYON. Worthy mother. How can I thank you?

HIGH PRIESTESS. You can't.

SOSIA. (*coming forward*) Oh noble, though persecuted lord. I see now that you are the true Amphitryon. Punish me, I deserve it. Beat me, whip me, stab me. Here, give me your sword, I'll do it myself.

AMPHITRYON. Scoundrel! What happened here since I left!

SOSIA. I have been barred from the palace, without a bite to eat. (*HIGH PRIESTESS and CITIZENS OF THEBES gasp. SOSIA sneaks a glance at DELORES' cleavage.*)

I have been de-Sosiasized . . . (*HIGH PRIESTESS and CITI-ZENS OF THEBES gasp again.*)

. . . just as you have been de-Amphitryonized! (*A third gasp.*)

High Priestess. Come, Citizens. Let us storm the palace at once!

All. Yes, come. Let us storm! Storm the palace! (etc.)

(*They all start for the palace in a line, led by the HIGH PRIEST-ESS. CITIZENS OF THEBES follow her. Next is SOSIA; last is AMPHITRYON. She stops suddenly, seeing someone approaching from the palace.*)

High Priestess. (*throwing her arms wide*) Hold!

Citizens of Thebes and Sosia. (*also throwing their arms wide*) Hold!

(*As he is putting on his helmet, AMPHITRYON is knocked back-wards and offstage by SOSIA's arm movement. A "boinnng" sound on the tympani accompanies AMPHITRYON's exit.*)

[MUSIC #28A — HAILS II]

High Priestess. (*sings*)
HAIL TO THE PRINCESS ALCMENE . . .
RADIANT AND PURE AS MOUNTAIN DEW!
Citizens of Thebes and Sosia.
HAIL TO THE PRINCESS ALCMENE . . .
WHO IS HALF SO VIRTUOUS AND TRUE?

(*ALCMENE, accompanied by CHARIS, enters from the palace and bows to the assemblage.*)

(*FANFARES. JUPITER and MERCURY enter from the pal-ace, as "AMPHITRYON" [TOM again, playing the double] enters, his helmet down over his face.*)

(*SOSIA takes his place by "AMPHITRYON;" MERCURY is next to JUPITER. The two sets of doubles face the rest of the company, their backs to the audience. "AMPHIT-RYON," facing upstage, raises his helmet, revealing his face to the assemblage. ALL gasp. "AMPHITRYON" lets the helmet drop down over his face.*)

HIGH PRIESTESS. Identical! Holy crap!

(*ALL look at DELORES as if to murder her. She shrinks back, mumbling her apologies.*)

ALCMENE. (*referring to "AMPHITRYON"*) But this is no god! If it was he who came to me last night . . . I *was* deceived by a mortal! Oh, how long must I suffer this uncertainty? (*She moves to CHARIS, who consoles her.*)

JUPITER. (*sotto voce to MERCURY*) Well . . . it won't be long now!

MERCURY. Father, you can't turn her into a constellation. You must reconsider!

(*JUPITER waves him off, and exits into the palace.*)

MERCURY. (*continued*) Good. Why don't you go inside, where we can talk?

(*MERCURY exits into palace.*)

DICK. Worthy mother, how are we to know which is the true Amphitryon?

HIGH PRIESTESS. May heaven grant me the wisdom to make the right decision! (*She looks to where JUPITER has exited, then back to "AMPHITRYON," gasping melodramatically. She gives them each a second look. Then:*)

One potato, two potato, three potato . . . (*pointing to "AMPHITRYON"*) Citizens, arrest *that* man!

(*"AMPHITRYON" runs off. CITIZENS OF THEBES rush after him, and drag back on the real AMPHITRYON, (who has stepped into the double's place when he ran offstage).*)

AMPHITRYON. (*removing his helmet*) Worthy mother! You too turn against me? Ye gods, is there no justice?

SOSIA. Worthy mother! How could you?

HIGH PRIESTESS. How could I not? The real husband must be the one the wife has recognized!

AMPHITRYON. She can't recognize him. The words will never cross her lips. Go on, ask her!

HIGH PRIESTESS. Princess Alcmene. Honey. Is that man in there Amphitryon, or what?

(*ALCMENE looks at the entrance to the palace. MERCURY has re-entered, and is now seen arguing with "JUPITER," whose back is to the audience.*)

[*NOTE: TOM plays the "JUPITER" double, with a wreath in place of "AMPHITRYON's" helmet.*]

(*ALCMENE looks at AMPHITRYON.*)

ALCMENE. (*shrugging, helplessly*) I don't know.
AMPHITRYON. See? I told you she couldn't do it. (*moving to embrace ALCMENE*) Darling!
ALCMENE. Fiend! Take your hands away from me! In darkness you deceived me, but by day, I see only too clearly. You pale in comparison with my true husband!
CHARIS. Worthy mother, put an end to this farce! Surely my mistress has suffered enough?
HIGH PRIESTESS. Yes, the matter is settled. (*pointing to AM-PHITRYON*) Take him away!

(*CITIZENS OF THEBES start to drag AMPHITRYON off. "JUPITER" enters the palace and MERCURY goes after him, still trying to appeal to his better nature.*)

AMPHITRYON. No! No, it's a trick. A trick, I tell you!
CHARIS. For shame, sir! My lady has made her choice. Would you denounce her now? Call her a liar before all of Thebes? Bring her to trial, as a willing adulteress! (*ALL gasp.*)
AMPHITRYON. Denounce her . . . as unfaithful? Nay, never that.

[MUSIC #28B — I KNOW MY WIFE UNDERSCORE]

(*AMPHITRYON draws himself up nobly, and speaks with great dignity.*)

AMPHITRYON. (*continued*) Hear me! Her every word is true as sunlight. If she says the other is her husband . . . though it denies my very existence . . . it must be so.
SOSIA. Sire! You would renounce your claim?
AMPHITRYON. Old friend, I did believe I was Amphitryon. In that, I may be mistaken. But in the purity of this woman's heart, my faith is unshakeable. (*to MERCURY, who has re-entered*)

Tell him he has won. I renounce claim to my lands, my wealth, my rank . . . and my wife. (*MUSIC out.*)
MERCURY. Sir, would you sacrifice everything?
AMPHITRYON. Aye.

[MUSIC #29 — TRIO]

AMPHITRYON. (*continued*) For in truth, I love her more than life itself. (*sings*)
BEFORE I SAY SHE LIES,
MAY THE STARS ABOVE GROW PALE.
MAY THE HEART WITHIN ME FAIL
BEFORE I SAY SHE LIES.

BEFORE I SAY SHE LIES,
I WOULD DRAW MY FINAL BREATH.
I WOULD GLADLY WELCOME DEATH
BEFORE I SAY SHE LIES . . .

(*AMPHITRYON draws his sword, and makes a tragic exit. ALCMENE moves forward.*)

ALCMENE. (*sings*)
OH NO! OH NO!
SUDDENLY MY HEART
IS GRIPPED WITH TERROR . . .
OH NO! OH NO!
OH NO NO NO NO NO . . .
I FEAR I MADE
A TINY ERROR . . .

THAT NOBLE MORTAL,
THAT WAS MY HUSBAND.
MAY JOVE FORGIVE ME,
I WAS WRONG.

(*MERCURY shoots a look to the offstage JUPITER, as if to say "Now look what you've done."*)

ALCMENE.	MERCURY.
THAT NOBLE MORTAL	LET THE HEART
WAS MY AMPHITRYON.	WITHIN HIM FAIL,
I SHOULD HAVE KNOWN IT	HE'LL NEVER SAY
ALL ALONG.	SHE LIES.

THAT NOBLE MORTAL,   BEFORE HE'LL SAY
THAT WAS MY HUSBAND: SHE LIES,
THAT WORTHY SOUL,   HE WOULD DRAW
THAT PRINCE OF MEN.   HIS FINAL BREATH.

THAT NOBLE MORTAL   HE WOULD GLADLY
WAS MY AMPHITRYON . . . WELCOME DEATH
THE WORLD WILL NEVER   BEFORE HE'LL SAY
SEE HIS LIKE AGAIN.   SHE LIES.

(*During the above, JUPITER has re-entered. ALCMENE falls
    to her knees, overcome with grief.*)

JUPITER.
GOOD GOD,
WHAT IS THIS I'M FEELING?
DEAR LORD,
SOMETHING'S VERY QUEER.
HOW ODD,
FEELING WHAT I'M FEELING.
BY JOVE!
DID I JUST SHED A TEAR?

JUPITER.	ALCMENE.	MERCURY.
GOOD GOD,	THAT NOBLE MORTAL,	BEFORE HE'LL SAY
HARD AS I AM TRYING,	THAT WAS MY HUSBAND:	SHE LIES,
THESE TEARS	THAT WORTHY SOUL,	HE WOULD DRAW
CAN NOT BE IGNORED.	THAT PRINCE OF MEN.	HIS FINAL BREATH.
GOOD GOD,	THAT NOBLE MORTAL	HE WOULD GLADLY
LOOK AT ME, I'M CRY-ING . . .	WAS MY AMPHIT-RYON . . .	WELCOME DEATH . . .

(*MUSIC continues under, as:*)

JUPITER. (*overcome with tears*) Mercury! What's come over
me?

MERCURY. (*rushing to JUPITER's side*) Don't be frightened,
Father. It's just another human emotion.

JUPITER. Good grief! What do they call *this* one?
MERCURY. Compassion! Isn't it wonderful?
JUPITER. I liked love better.
ALCMENE. Please. If that was my Amphitryon, . . . (*MUSIC out.*) . . . then who—?
JUPITER. Good heavens, lady. Haven't you gotten it yet?

[MUSIC #29A—HEAVENLY CHORDS]

(*Three loud, majestic chords are heard. Lights dim, as JUPITER is bathed in a celestial light. ALL back away, awed by the sight, cowering reverentially as if in a biblical movie. ALCMENE runs off to join her husband, and TOM joins the group, now dressed as a CITIZEN OF THEBES.*)

[MUSIC #30—MINE EYES HAVE SEEN THE LORD]

CHARIS. (*gazing at JUPITER*) . . . Sosia, look! Look! (*sings, with great reverence:*)
GLORY BE,
I'VE SEEN THE LORD!
WITH MY OWN EYES
I'VE SEEN THE LORD . . .

Hallelujah!

I EVEN HEARD THE ANGELS SING.
LET HISTORY RECORD:
MINE EYES HAVE SEEN THE LORD.

(*SOSIA moves forward, caught up in the spirit of the moment, and testifies as if at a prayer meeting.*)

SOSIA.
GLORY BE,
LOOK AT THAT FACE.
I TESTIFY
I'VE SEEN THAT FACE.

I THOUGHT THAT I'D SEEN EVERYTHING
BUT THIS TIME I WAS FLOORED.

CHARIS and SOSIA.
MINE EYES HAVE SEEN THE LORD.

(*CITIZENS OF THEBES and HIGH PRIESTESS join CHARIS
    and SOSIA in a rousing spiritual.*)

CHORUS.
GLORY BE,
I'VE SEEN THE LORD!
CHARIS and SOSIA.
GLORY BE,
I'VE SEEN THE LORD!
CHORUS.
WITH MY OWN EYES,
I'VE SEEN THE LORD!
JUPITER.
I AM THE LORD,
I AM THE LORD!
CHARIS, SOSIA and CHORUS.
I EVEN HEARD THE ANGELS SING.
LET HISTORY RECORD:
MINE EYES HAVE SEEN THE LORD.

MY FAITH HAS BEEN RESTORED.
MY EYES
HAVE
SEEN
THE
LORD . . .
(*JUPITER and MERCURY move to center.*)
MERCURY. (*proudly*) That's my Dad!

(*Applause. ALCMENE re-enters, frantic.*)

ALCMENE. Please! Amphitryon appears near death!
JUPITER. Fear not. He shall revive shortly.

[MUSIC #30A — UNDERSCORE]

(*A collective sigh of relief. JUPITER addresses ALCMENE.*)

JUPITER. (*continued*) My child. It has pleased Jupiter . . . along with his son Mercury . . . (*ALCMENE turns to MERCURY; they shake hands.*) . . . to visit your house. If my thanks do not suffice, name your wish and it shall be granted.

ALCMENE. Forgive me, but I am not satisfied. Please, grant us the boon of a child, to carry on my husband's name?

JUPITER. (*a bit sheepishly*) It has already been arranged. You shall have a son, and he shall be called Hercules—the greatest hero to walk the earth. (*MUSIC out.*)

(*ALL cheer and applaud. CHARIS comes forward, tapping JU-PITER on the shoulder, a bit shyly.*)

CHARIS. Uh . . . what about me? I've been good. What about my reward?

JUPITER. Your reward?

SOSIA. Oh, Charis. You can't *really* believe these two clowns are gods? (*MERCURY and JUPITER exchange glances, then each raises an arm to the heavens. A tremendous display of lightning and thunder. After it subsides:*)

Can I have your autograph?

MERCURY. Father, what about that new constellation you arranged for? There'll be an empty spot up in the heavens.

JUPITER. By thunder, we can't have that! I'll have to take Alcmene back to heaven with me after all!

(*ALL protest. HIGH PRIESTESS rushes forward.*)

HIGH PRIESTESS. Fear not, fear not! I, High Priestess of Thebes, will gladly make the supreme sacrifice, and take her place in the pantheon of stars!

ALCMENE. Holy mother. Would you really?

HIGH PRIESTESS. Try and stop me!

[MUSIC #31—HEAVEN ON EARTH (FINALE)]

(*MUSIC under. ALCMENE turns to JUPITER.*)

ALCMENE. Then I suppose this is farewell? Forever?

JUPITER. Please, Alcmene. You pierce my heart. To an immortal, forever is a very long time. (*sings*)
LADY . . . LADY . . .

I WAS NOT PREPARED.
WHO DREAMED I'D FIND LOVE
THE NIGHT WE SHARED . . .
>ALCMENE.
THE NIGHT WE SHARED . . .
>JUPITER.
HEAVEN ON EARTH?
>ALCMENE.
HEAVEN ON EARTH!
>JUPITER.
HEAVEN ON EARTH!
>ALCMENE.
HEAVEN ON EARTH!
>JUPITER.
HOW WE TOOK TO THE SKY . . .
>ALCMENE.
HOW WE FLEW, YOU AND I . . .
>JUPITER and ALCMENE.
HOW YOU TURNED MY WORLD AROUND!

(*JUPITER moves to kiss ALCMENE goodbye, thinks better of it, and gives her a paternal kiss on the forehead.*)

>JUPITER and ALCMENE.
LOST IN YOUR ARMS I FOUND
HEAVEN ON EARTH . . .

(*MERCURY exits, with DELORES. JUPITER starts to follow them, turns back for a final look at ALCMENE, and exits.*)

(*ALL gaze at the heavens. The sky is full of stars.*)

CURTAIN

BOWS

[MUSIC #32 — BOWS]

(*TOM, DICK and HORACE take the first bow, together. The principals each take solo bows. The order of bows is at the discretion of the producer, except that DELORES must come next to last, now sporting a magnificent white fur coat. The last bow is reserved for the actor playing the roles of JUPI-TER and AMPHITRYON. He wears his wreath, and carries his helmet under his arm.)*

(*The ENTIRE COMPANY sings:*)

ENTIRE COMPANY.
SHE'LL APPEAR ON THE SCENE
RIGHT IN BETWEEN
LEO AND CAPRICORN.
ONLY MOMENTS FROM NOW,
SHE'LL BE TAKING HER BOW.
(*COMPANY splits left and right.*)
TONIGHT, A STAR IS . . .

(*Tympani roll. A huge red banner flies in center stage. It bears the legend "FURS BY MURRIER THE FURRIER." DE-LORES waves excitedly at MURRAY, out in the house.*)

BORN!!!

(*ENTIRE COMPANY bows, and the lights dim.*)

[MUSIC #33 — EXIT MUSIC]

PROP LIST

Stage Left
Flower (for JUPITER)
Stick (for MERCURY)
Breastplate (for DELORES)
Rubber chickens (2, for CHARIS)
Silver lamé capes (4, for CHARIS, MERCURY, JUPITER &
    SOSIA)
Canes (4, for CHARIS, MERCURY, JUPITER & SOSIA)
Sequinned hats (for CHARIS, MERCURY, JUPITER &
    SOSIA)

Stage Right
Helmet with plume (for JUPITER)
Cigarette (for CHARIS)
Jewelled belt with initial J (for ALCMENE)
Garden rake (for SOSIA)
Pouch with initial A (for SOSIA)
Silver lamé capes (4, for ALCMENE, TOM, DICK &
    HORACE)
Canes (4, for ALCMENE, TOM, DICK & HORACE)
Sequinned hats (for ALCMENE, TOM, DICK & HORACE)

Personal props
Rose (for CHARIS)
Handkerchief (for CHARIS)
Sword (for JUPITER/AMPHITRYON)
Cupid's bow (for DELORES)

COSTUME PLOT & NOTES

The basic idea to keep in mind when mounting *Olympus On My Mind* is that the play is a constant juxtaposition of contemporary elements with classical elements. This is made evident in the book, lyrics and score, and must be followed through in the direction, acting and design. The obvious visual contrast is between the "play characters" and DELORES; however, every costume in the show should somehow pit "modern" against "ancient Greek" to varying extents.

JUPITER/AMPHITRYON

He should be the most classic-looking of the "play characters." The only modern elements of his costume in the original production were in the decoration, such as the border of his cape, which mixed Keith Haring-type hieroglyphics with a classic Greek key motif. JUPITER wears a golden olive wreath on his head; AMPHITRYON wears or carries a helmet. The actor does not have time for any more elaborate change.

Classical chiton (tunic) ending mid-thigh
Armor worn over chiton, with shirt made up of lappets
Cape
Greaves (armor protecting shins)
Armoured wrist guards
Elegant gold sandals
Sword and scabbard
Short shorts to wear under chiton (same color as chiton)
Golden olive wreath (as JUPITER)
Helmet with plume (as AMPHITRYON); helmet should mask
 most of face when worn
Old Jupiter cloak and beard (when JUPITER is discovered be-
 hind scrim after opening number)
Silver lamé drapery and sequinned top hat for "A Star Is Born"

ALCMENE

She must be stunningly beautiful. ALCMENE is vulnerable, but remember that she is a married woman, not a Vestal virgin. We gave her a slinky, Vicky Tiel-type strapless gown with some diaphanous Greek drapery.

Primitive-pleated strapless gown with removeable drape hanging
 off shoulder

92

Matching golden belt and diadem
Gold earrings
Gold high-heeled evening sandals
Second belt, jewelled with the initial "J" on back
Silk robe for scene following the 17-hour night with JUPITER
Silver lamé drapery and sequinned top hat for "A Star is Born"

MERCURY and SOSIA

MERCURY and SOSIA are "doubles," yet must be as opposite
as doubles can be. SOSIA is a miserable-looking "schlep" and
MERCURY is a handsome young Greek god. Their costumes
should be the same fabric and cut, but SOSIA's should fit him
terribly and be totally unflattering while MERCURY's must be
extremely flattering and well-fitting. Our palette was from Greek
vase paintings (golden ochre, terra cotta, and black), and what
was a flat color on SOSIA's trim and accessories became a corre-
sponding metallic on MERCURY's (e.g. metallic copper instead
of terra cotta) to show MERCURY's "godliness" coming through
in another way.

SOSIA

Tunic/shirt with Greek key trim
Baggy shorts, made of same fabric as tunic
Braided cord belt that ties
Headband
Rustic sandals
Pouch with velcroed seal rigged to break open
Silver lamé drapery and sequinned top hat for "A Star is Born"

MERCURY

Tunic/shirt with metallic Greek key trim
Trim shorts made of same fabric as tunic
Belt made of braided metallic cords
Golden headband with gold wings behind ears
Gold leather hi-top athletic shoes with gold wings attached at
    ankles
Silver lamé drapery and sequinned top hat for "A Star is Born"

CHARIS

She is the ugliest woman in Thebes. CHARIS is prim, proper,
and conservative. How do you get across the idea of "old fashioned" when everyone else is dressed in classic Greek? We used

more archaic Greek elements rather than Hellenistic, and threw in some caveman accessories. CHARIS must go through a complete changeover for "At Liberty In Thebes." Her underwear can be almost anything, as long as it is funny (rather than sexy). Keep in mind that CHARIS must be able to gracefully get out of her overgarment onstage in about 2 seconds, and then must be able to get back into it later onstage in a maximum of about 20 or 30 seconds.

Doric chiton with peplos (overfold) trimmed with archaic
    Gorgon heads, rigged to open at shoulders and fall to ground
Macrame belt and hairbands
Cavewoman sandals
Bone earrings and long bone in hair
Corset with fringe (for "At Liberty in Thebes")
Boxer shorts with silly print, trimmed in fringe (for "At Liberty
    in Thebes")
Silver lamé drapery and sequinned top hat for "A Star is Born"

THE CHORUS

TOM, DICK and HORACE should bridge the visual gap between the "play characters" and DELORES. We gave them very contemporary-looking basic costumes that could look more Greek with the addition of some drapery. The basic costumes were white with an overall silkscreened pattern of Greek column capitals in blue, wine red, and golden yellow, and then each had a "cape" lined and trimmed in one of those three colors. These were semi-circular capes that were engineered so that they could be worn in the back hanging off both shoulders for the "Generals' Pandemonium" or could alternately be worn hanging off one shoulder, with the center of the cape underneath the opposite arm creating a look of generic Greek drapery. The other chorus costume problem is the fact that each of the three needs two pairs of identical sandals that can be danced in: one pair with taps and one without.

TOM

Sleeveless square neck tunic/shirt
Pants of same fabric, rolled up to right below knee
Shorts of same fabric hemmed about 1" lower than hem of tunic
    (for "At Liberty in Thebes")
Wide leather belt
2 pairs of matching sandals, one with taps (for "The Gods on
    Tap") one with dance rubber (for rest of show)

Greek looking drapery hanging from left shoulder and passing
   under right arm (may be rigged to double as DELORES's cape
   in "Generals' Pandemonium")
Silver lamé drapery and sequinned top hat for "A Star is Born"
Exact and complete copy of JUPITER/AMPHITRYON's
   costume: chiton, armor, cape, greaves, wrist guards,
   helmet—to be worn when TOM is playing the "double" for
   AMPHITRYON.

DICK

Tunic/shirt, pants, shorts, belt, and 2 pairs of sandals, same
   as TOM's
Horn-rimmed glasses, worn througout the show
Greek looking drapery like TOM's, but rigged to be also worn as
   a cape for "Generals' Pandemonium" (or else a separate cape
   may be worn for that number)
Military helmet (for "Generals' Pandemonium")
Silver lamé drapery and sequinned top hat for "A Star is Born"

HORACE

All the same items as DICK, minus the horn-rimmed glasses

DELORES

The character of DELORES is played as though she came into
the production well after the show was written, designed, and
directed. She is a complete intrusion into the piece, and should
always look out of place. It should appear as if she had her own
costume designer, who fashioned all her costumes, with practi-
cally no regard to the rest of the play or anything or anyone else
on stage. She needs to be a visual joke every time she enters. Being the wife of "Murray the Furrier," she models a new fur piece
in each of her scenes. Her costumes should definitely look as if
more money than taste went into them. (Not too much money,
though. DELORES's costumes should be sequinned rather than
beaded, even if you can afford beading; and remember, all of
MURRAY's fur pieces are second-hand).

Her costumes become progressively more outrageous within the
context of the show. In "A Star is Born," she needs a not-too
tasteful or sophisticated imitation of a Bob Mackie gown. In the

final scene, she misses the boat completely. Her High Priestess costume looks as if she were a priestess from the Egyptian city of Thebes, instead of the Greek city of Thebes. Her final white fur coat, worn in the bows, should be a knockout.

DELORES changes at every entrance; costumes are listed according to musical numbers.

"Welcome to Greece"

Strapless bodice with Ionic capital embroidered in sequins
    (the two volutes of the capital are positioned similarly to the
    wings of the eagle on Wonder Woman's costume)
Dance trunks
Skirt made of strings of gold beads (like a beaded curtain)
Silver or rhinestone evening or ballroom sandals
Silver sequinned headband
Sequinned headdress shaped like a Corinthian capital
Rhinestone earrings and bracelets
Fur muff

"The Gods on Tap"

Silver tap shoes replace sandals
Fur fling and fur pillbox hat replace fur muff and capital
    headdress

"Love— What A Concept"

Red pointe shoes replace tap shoes
Red heart-shaped headdress replaces fur pillbox hat
White fur stole replaces fur fling
Tutu skirt replaces beaded skirt
Carries Cupid's bow

"Enter the Husband"

Same costume as "Welcome to Greece"
New, blue fox stole

"Back So Soon"

New animal-shaped fur (with head and tail) replaces blue fox
    stole. Fur piece is draped tragically over her head.

"Jupiter Slept Here"

Sequinned tube top
New "beaded curtain" skirt
Fur stole with many paws and tails hanging off
Same shoes and dance trunks

"Back to the Play"

Same as "Welcome to Greece"

"Enter the Husband (reprise)"

Same, but without fur or headdress

"Generals' Pandemonium"

Over her basic costume, DELORES wears:

Muscled Roman breastplate (male) with pink maribou trim,
    jewelled nipples and navel, sequin and rhinestone decorative
    motifs
Gold sequin wrist guards
Cape
Helmet, same as DICK and HORACE, but with large bird of
    prey perched on top, sporting colorful "eye-catching" plumes

"A Star Is Born"

Fully sequinned long strapless gown, a la Bob Mackie
Hollywood starlet wig (red)
Long silver gloves with stars and rhinestones scattered over
Rhinestone earrings and necklace
Full length fur coat (covers her dress)

"Final Sequence" (High Priestess of Thebes)

Sleeveless gold V-neck leotard
Leopard skin draped over leotard
Gold hip belt with long hanging section center front and strings
    of gold beads swagged all around
Black Cleopatra wig
Cleopatra-type headdress with golden asps, etc.
Rhinestone earrings and necklace from previous "Star" costume

"Curtain Call"

Full length white fur coat, worn over High Priestess Costume.

A SPECIAL NOTE ON *"A STAR IS BORN"*:

This number must look very different from everything that has gone before in the show. We used black and silver, neither of which had been seen previously, except in small amounts. Keep in mind that this is somewhat of a humiliating experience for the "play characters," who have been forced to become back-up chorus members to this bimbo DELORES. Their costumes should humiliate them further.

Notes by Steven Jones

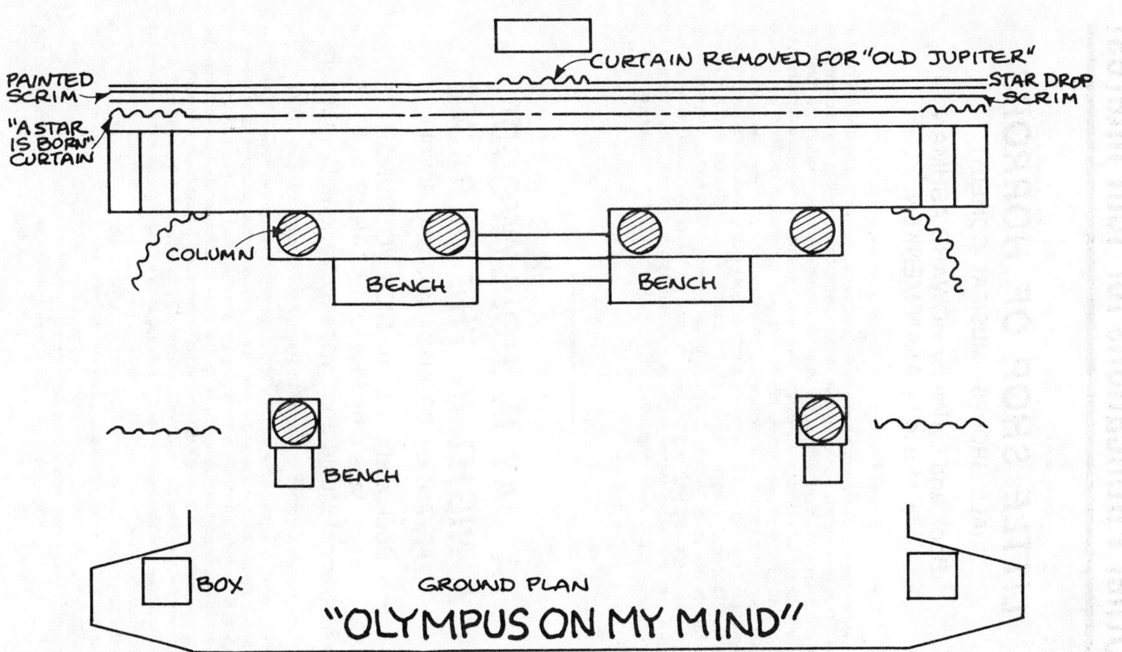

Set design by Christopher Stapleton

Other Publications for Your Interest

LITTLE SHOP OF HORRORS
(ALL GROUPS—MUSICAL COMEDY)
Book and Lyrics by HOWARD ASHMAN
Music by ALAN MENKEN

5 men, 4 women—Combination Interior/Exterior

Based on the film of the same name by Roger Corman. Screenplay by Charles Griffith. Look Out, here comes Audrey II! Live, and in Living Color, thrill to the excitement as Seymour, lowly assistant to florist Mr. Mushnik, desperately tries to satisfy the voracious craving for human flesh of the unearthly plant which seems to grow before our very eyes, singing and dancing its way into our hearts—literally. Sigh as Seymour tries to win the love of Audrey I (also known as Audrey), who also works in the shop. Her sado-masochistic dentist (isn't that redundant?) boyfriend becomes quite a tasty meal for the plant: but not its last! Suspense! Laughter! Chills! Music! Drama! And, a "60's Girl-Group" Chorus! "Adorable little spoof."—W.W. Daily. "Gleefully gruesome. This horticultural horror will have you screaming with laughter."—N.Y. Post. "It leaves the audience feeling just like Audrey II between victims—ravenous for more."—N.Y. Times. This long-running off-Broadway success was originally produced by the excellent W.P.A. Theatre in NYC.

(#666)

A DAY IN HOLLYWOOD/
A NIGHT IN THE UKRAINE
(ADVANCED GROUPS—MUSICAL REVUE)
Book and Lyrics by DICK VOSBURGH
Music by FRANK LAZARUS
Additional Music and Lyrics by Various Composers

4 men, 4 women, 1 pianist on stage, 2 pianists backstage—2 Sets

"Hollywood" is a marvelous nostalgic spoof of Hollywood and the movies of the 1930s that will delight both those who remember it and those too young to have known it. "Ukraine" is the comedy the Marx Brothers didn't make, but could have. It is ever-new, ever-fresh Marx Brothers updated and transformed into comic symbols of their time. This is a "musical double feature" and like the old movie double-header there is no connection between the two acts. But together it is fascinatingly successful. "The puns have wings . . . you leave the theatre with the dizzy feeling of having witnessed a super, impossibly professional senior-class spring show. Not a bed feeling, at all."—N.Y. Daily News. "It is crazy, zany magic . . . a smashing show, classy, sassy nostalgia."—N.Y. Post. "Act One is a splendidly funny and remarkably clever entertainment, Act Two has inspired lunacy, impeccable foolishness and perfectly hilarious nonsense."—WCBS-TV2. "A real winner . . . consists of two extended sketches, both gems."—Wall Street Journal.

A Day in Hollywood/A Night in The Ukraine (#6658)
A Night in The Ukraine (#16057)

OLYMPUS ON MY MIND

A Musical

Suggested by "Amphitryon" by Heinrich Von Kleist

Book and Lyrics by
Barry Harman

Music by
Grant Sturiale

*Original Production
Directed by*

Barry Harman

Originally presented by
Harve Brosten and Mainstage Productions, Ltd.

No part of this book may be reproduced, stored in a retrieval system, or transmitted in any form, by any means, including mechanical, electronic, photocopying, recording, or otherwise, without the prior written permission of the publisher.

SAMUEL FRENCH, INC.

45 WEST 25TH STREET   NEW YORK 10010
7623 SUNSET BOULEVARD   HOLLYWOOD 90046
LONDON   *TORONTO*